Diagnostic Classification: 0-3

Diagnostic Classification of Mental Health and Developmental Disorders of Infancy and Early Childhood

ZERO TO THREE: National Center for Infants, Toddlers, and Families

ZERO TO THREE: National Center for Infants, Toddlers, and Families is the only national non-profit organization dedicated solely to improving the chances for healthy physical, cognitive, emotional, and social development of infants, toddlers, and their families.

Established in 1977, ZERO TO THREE is committed to:

• exercising leadership in developing and communicating a national vision of the importance of the first three years of life and of the importance of early intervention and prevention to healthy growth and development;

• focusing attention on the quality of infants' and toddlers' major relationships and on children's day-to-day experiences within these relationships;

• developing a broader understanding of how services for infants, toddlers, and their families are best provided; and

• promoting training in keeping with that understanding.

Preface

Knowledge about infant mental health and development has grown exponentially in the last two decades. Through systematic observation, research and clinical intervention, a more sophisticated understanding has emerged of the factors that contribute to adaptive and maladaptive patterns of development and of the meaning of individual differences in infancy. This knowledge has led to an increasing awareness of the importance of prevention and early treatment in creating or restoring favorable conditions for the young child's development and mental health. Timely assessment and accurate diagnosis can provide the foundation for effective intervention before early deviations become consolidated into maladaptive patterns of functioning.

The diagnostic framework presented in *Diagnostic Classification of Mental Health and Developmental Disorders of Infancy and Early Childhood* (*Diagnostic Classification: 0-3*) seeks to address the need for a systematic, developmentally based approach to the classification of mental health and developmental difficulties in the first four years of life. It is designed to complement existing medical and developmental frameworks for understanding mental health and developmental problems in the earliest years.

Diagnostic Classification: 0-3 categorizes emotional and behavioral patterns that represent significant deviations from normative development in the earliest years of life. Some of the categories presented represent new formulations of mental health and developmental difficulties. Other categories describe the earliest manifestations of mental health problems which have been identified among older children and adults but have not been fully described in infants and young children. In infancy and early childhood, these problems may have different characteristics, and prognosis may be more optimistic if effective early intervention can occur.

Diagnostic Classification: 0-3 is the product of the multidisciplinary Diagnostic Classification Task Force which was established in 1987 by ZERO TO THREE : National Center for Infants, Toddlers, and Families, an organization representing interdisciplinary professional leadership in the field of infant development and mental health. Task Force members include leading clinicians and researchers from infant centers throughout the United States, Canada, and Europe. The goal of the Task Force has been to collect information about infants and toddlers with clinical problems requiring diagnosis and intervention. During the past six years, the Task Force has built a data base through systematic reporting of cases from various centers working with infants and families. The data base served as the foundation for case discussion and for the identification of recurring patterns of behavioral problems. Descriptive categories were developed as a result of these discussions, and each category became progressively more refined through consideration of new cases that presented challenges to the initial formulation.

From 1987 to 1990, Task Force members, meeting twice a year in Washington, D.C. and communicating throughout the year by telephone, fax, and mail, formulated an initial set of diagnostic categories through expert consensus. In 1990, the Task Force expanded to include additional participants, representing a variety of disciplines, who helped to further refine the diagnostic categories and to broaden the number and types of settings in which cases were collected for the Diagnostic Classification Task Force data base. The Task Force continues to meet and collects descriptive and clinical data on infants and families who come for services, the types of problems they are experiencing, and the services they receive. The data collection form used by Task Force members and guidelines for its use are available for clinicians interested in participating in the ongoing data collection which will provide an expanding empirical base for further refinement of this diagnostic system.

The ZERO TO THREE: National Center for Infants, Toddlers, and Families Diagnostic Classification Task Force welcomes communication about Diagnostic Classification: 0-3, including case studies that support or challenge the classifications presented here, and indications of a wish to participate in the ongoing data collection and dialogue to refine and revise the classification system. Send communications to Emily Fenichel, Associate Director, **ZERO TO THREE**, 2000 M Street, NW, Suite 200, Washington, DC 20036-3307, (202) 638-1144, fax (202) 638-0851.

Acknowledgments

Diagnostic Classification: 0-3 represents the work of many people with a passionate desire to understand the complexities of development in the earliest years of life. Three individuals deserve the special appreciation of the Diagnostic Classification Task Force and of all who find this volume helpful. They are the late Reginald Lourie, Founding Member and former Chairman of the Board of the National Center for Clinical Infant Programs, the late Sally Provence, Founding Member and former President of ZERO TO THREE/National Center for Clinical Infant Programs, and Kathryn Barnard, former chair of the Research Facilitation Committee and President of ZERO TO THREE/National Center for Clinical Infant Programs. The research and clinical leadership of Drs. Lourie, Provence and Barnard are well known; their steadfast, continuing support of the challenging collective work of the Task Force, from its very beginnings, is part of their many contributions to the well-being of very young children and their families.

ZERO TO THREE/National Center for Clinical Infant Programs is grateful to the A.L. Mailman Family Foundation for generous and timely support for the publication and dissemination of *Diagnostic Classification of Mental Health and Developmental Disorders of Infancy and Early Childhood.*

Stanley I. Greenspan, M.D., Chair

Serena Wieder, Ph.D., Co-Chair and Clinical Director

The ZERO TO THREE/National Center for Clinical Infant Programs

Diagnostic Classification Task Force

Members

Ongoing Task Force Participants

Editor

Staff

The Diagnostic Classification Task Force appreciates the contribution of individuals who attended selected meetings of the Task Force and made suggestions, and of the parents and clinicians who reviewed earlier drafts of this manual.

Table of Contents

Case Vignettes   84

In order to accommodate those who wish to first read and diagnose cases independently, cases are not identified by category here.

Readers who wish to identify cases representing specific categories should consult the index to primary diagnoses of cases on page 134

Index to Primary Diagnoses of Cases   134

Introduction

Formulating categories for the classification of mental health and developmental disorders manifested early in life serves a number of purposes:

• A classification system provides a way for clinicians and researchers to organize their observations.

• A classification system assists clinicians in assessment and in formulating recommendations for intervention or further monitoring.

• A classification system provides a common language that clinicians and researchers can use to communicate with one another, to collect systematic data on various disorders, and, over time, to improve understanding of types of disorders, the factors that influence their course, and the components and effectiveness of interventions.

• A classification system provides an initial framework from which further refinements and changes can be made.

Discussions of diagnostic categories can be most helpful if they identify challenges to be overcome in the context of an understanding of adaptive coping and development. Understanding both adaptive capacities and challenges is part of the essential foundation for planning and implementing effective interventions. Diagnostic categories should not be used to "label" a child or to distract attention from positive, coping capacities and the inherent capacity of human beings to grow and develop. Diagnostic categories, rather, should encourage greater precision in describing a child's challenges and abilities; this precision will guide potentially more effective intervention strategies.

There are many possible approaches to developing a classification system. From an academic point of view, such a system would strive for symmetry. It would be descriptive, etiological, or based on pathophysiologic processes. In the history of medicine, however, where the focus is on describing phenomena as they are encountered in natural (as compared to laboratory) settings, classification systems have evolved asymmetrically, based on evolving understanding of the conditions encountered. In medicine, diagnoses tend initially to be descriptive of a group of symptoms or a pattern of behavior. As underlying pathophysiologic processes are understood, descriptive categories tend to become more functional and physiologically based. Eventually, as etiological factors are understood, diagnostic categories reflect causative factors. Diagnoses of "headache" or "low back pain" may be either descriptive (of symptoms) or physiologically based, depending on whether or not diagnostic studies reveal compromise in the patient's physiologic processes. "Strep throat," however, is an etiological diagnosis, made after identifying the presence of streptococci, a bacterial organism known to cause infection.

Reflecting our current state of knowledge, the diagnostic categories presented in this manual are descriptive — that is, they record presenting patterns of symptoms and behaviors. Some of the categories (for example, those involving trauma) imply potential etiological factors; some (for example, regulatory disorders) imply pathophysiological processes. However, at the moment, all that can be stated is that associations have been observed between some of these symptoms and processes (for example, between a traumatic event and a group of symptoms, or between a sensory or motor pattern and a group of symptoms). Only further research will establish possible pathophysiological and/or etiological links among these observed phenomena.

In approaching its goals, the Diagnostic Classification Task Force considered a number of methodological approaches. Because study of mental health and developmental disorders in infancy and early childhood constitutes a new clinical field, Task Force members believed that creation of a diagnostic classification system should proceed by building up a data base of cases for discussion by experts. Through consensus of clinical and research experts, preliminary conceptualizations were formulated. Additional data were collected and analyzed, leading to changes and refinements in the initial system. This process will be ongoing, in order to provide an expanding empirical base for further refinement of the diagnostic system presented here.

In any scientific enterprise, but particularly in a new field, a healthy tension exists between the desire to analyze findings from systematic research before offering even initial conceptualizations, and the need to disseminate preliminary conceptualizations so that they can serve as a basis for collecting systematic data, which can lead to more empirically based efforts. The history of such efforts reflects the need for a balanced interaction between these two positions. The development of *Diagnostic Classification: 0-3* represents an important first step: the presentation of expert consensus-based categorizations of mental health and developmental disorders in the early years of life. As an evolving framework this conceptualization is not intended to include all possible conditions or disorders. It is an initial guide for clinicians and researchers to facilitate clinical diagnosis and planning, as well as communication and further research. It is not intended to have legal or non-clinical applications.

Clinical approaches to assessment and diagnosis

Many different assumptions and theories contribute to our approach to diagnosis and treatment. These assumptions come from both clinical practice and research. Developmental, psychodynamic, family systems, relationship, and attachment theory inform our work, as do observations of the ways infants organize their experience, infant/caregiver interaction patterns, temperament, regulatory patterns, and individual differences in many domains of development.

Assessment and diagnosis must be guided by the awareness that all infants are participants in relationships. These relationships exist, usually, within families, and families themselves are part of the larger community and culture. At the same time, all infants have their own developmental progression and show individual differences in their motor, sensory, language, cognitive, affective and interactive patterns.

While self-evident, these facts are hard to take into account simultaneously. Regardless of their desire to be balanced, most clinicians will favor one or another theory or approach, or concentrate their attention on particular developmental domains or aspects of the caregiving environment. For example, one clinician may focus her attention primarily on the mother's projection of feelings about herself, or from an earlier relationship, onto her infant, even though the clinician's assessment may also describe how the infant's constitutional-maturational pattern in part inspires the mother's projections. Another clinician may focus on how the infant's over-reactivity to sensation sets up an interactive pattern in which the parent feels rejected and vacillates between intrusiveness and withdrawal. A third clinician may see the relationship between caregiver and infant as primary, considering the constitutional-maturational and family patterns as secondary. Still other clinicians will see the family system, or a particular aspect of the caregiver-child interaction, or environmental stressors as most critical.

In conducting research, we may occasionally have the luxury of studying single variables in a systematic effort to determine their relationship to a particular aspect of development. In clinical practice, however, a systematic approach must be a comprehensive approach. Each child and each family is different. The clinician cannot know in advance which variables are exerting a dominant influence on development, or how relationships between and among variables are affecting the child and family.

Any intervention or treatment program should be based on as complete an understanding of the child and family's circumstances as is possible to achieve. However, it is not uncommon for clinicians to give lip service to the importance of a comprehensive approach to diagnosis, but then to address "favorite" variables in great detail, while giving only cursory regard to other influences on development (e.g., an evaluation consisting of a six-page description of the family system and a single sentence categorizing the infant's pattern of interaction with his caregiver). Clinicians may also be tempted to avoid assessing those areas of functioning where the constructs or research tools are less well developed, or which represent gaps in their own training.

Although these temptations are understandable, it is the responsibility of any clinician who is charged with doing a full diagnostic work-up and planning an appropriate intervention program to take into account **all** the relevant areas of a child's functioning, using state-of-the-art knowledge in each area. These areas include:

- presenting symptoms and behaviors;
- developmental history — past and current affective, language, cognitive, motor, sensory, family, and interactive functioning;
- family functioning and cultural and community patterns;
- parents as individuals;
- caregiver-infant (child) relationship and interactive patterns;
- the infant's constitutional-maturational characteristics; and
- affective, language, cognitive, motor and sensory patterns.

In addition, it is important to consider the family's psychosocial and medical history, the history of the pregnancy and delivery, and current environmental conditions and stressors.

The process of gaining an understanding of how each area of functioning is developing for an infant or toddler usually requires a number of sessions. A few questions to parents or caregiver about each area may be appropriate for screening, but not for a full evaluation. A full evaluation usually requires a minimum of three to five sessions of 45 or more minutes each. A complete evaluation will usually involve taking the history, direct observation of functioning (i.e., of family and parental dynamics, caregiver-infant relationship and interaction patterns, the infant's constitutional—maturational characteristics, and language, cognitive and affective patterns), and hands-on interactive assessment of the infant, including assessment of sensory reactivity and processing, motor tone and planning, language, cognition, and affective expression. Standardized developmental assessments, if needed, should always build on the clinical process described above. They may be indicated when they are the most effective way to answer specific questions and when the child is sufficiently interactive and can respond to the requirements of the test.

The result of such a comprehensive evaluation should lead to preliminary notions about:

1. The nature of the infant's or child's difficulties, as well as her or his strengths; the level of the child's overall adaptive capacity; and functioning in the major areas of development, including social-emotional, relationships, cognitive, language, sensory and motor abilities in comparison to age-expected developmental patterns.

2. The relative contribution of the different areas assessed (family relationships, interactive patterns, constitutional-maturational patterns, stress, etc.) to the child's difficulties and competencies.

3. A comprehensive treatment or preventive intervention plan to deal with 1) and 2) above.

A clinician conducting a diagnostic evaluation and formulating an intervention plan should have considerable experience in assessing all the areas of functioning described above and in integrating the assessment findings into a cohesive formulation. If necessary, colleagues with the expertise to help assess specific areas of functioning should be called upon as needed. When a team, rather than a single clinician, is responsible for conducting an assessment and formulating the diagnosis and intervention plan, at least one member of the team should have considerable experience in integrating the different elements of the assessment into an integrated understanding of the nature of the difficulty and the type of intervention(s) most likely to be helpful.

Part of this expertise involves understanding infant/caregiver interaction patterns and the relationship between the interaction patterns and adaptive and maladaptive emotional and developmental patterns. In addition, this expertise involves understanding how constitutional and maturational variations — including individual differences in motor, sensory, language, cognitive and affective patterns — influence infant/caregiver interaction patters and related adaptive and maladaptive emotional and developmental patterns. It also involves understanding the influence of parental, family, cultural and community patterns on infant/caregiver patterns and related emotional developmental patterns.

A comprehensive assessment as described above may occur in many different settings. Settings that are strong in only some areas of assessment and intervention should obtain additional expertise through engaging additional staff or consultation, or through training existing staff. In this way a variety of settings may be able to conduct truly comprehensive approaches to assessment and intervention with infants and young children.

An overview of the classification system

Diagnostic Classification: 0-3 proposes a provisional multiaxial classification system. We refer to the classification system as provisional because we assume that categories may change as more knowledge accumulates. The diagnostic framework consists of the following:

Axis I: Primary Classification

Axis II: Relationship Classification

Axis III: Physical, Neurological, Developmental and Mental Health
   Disorders or Conditions (described in other classification systems)

Axis IV: Psychosocial Stress

Axis V: Functional Emotional Developmental Level

The axes in this system are not intended to be entirely symmetrical with such other systems as DSM IV and ICD-10 because this system, in dealing with infants and young children, focuses on developmental issues. Dynamic processes, such as relationship and developmentally based conceptualizations of adaptive patterns (i.e., functional emotional developmental level) are therefore of central importance.

Use of the system will provide the clinician with a **diagnostic profile** of an infant or toddler. Such a diagnostic profile focuses the clinician's attention on the various factors that are contributing to the infant's difficulties as well as areas in which intervention may be needed.

Diagnostic Classification: 0-3 is intended to complement other frameworks and therefore is not intended to include categories for every type of developmental or mental health disorder. Because many existing frameworks for mental health and developmental problems have not focused in depth on the first three to four years of life, they have not included a comprehensive system for classifying problems in this early age range. This is in part due to the pioneering nature of clinical work with infants, young children and families. This diagnostic framework, therefore, describes: 1) types of problems or behaviors not addressed in other classification approaches, and 2) the earliest manifestations of problems and behavior that are described in other systems for somewhat older children and adults. Where we have described the earlier manifestations of a disorder described in an existing classification system, we have attempted to use identifying terms similar to those used in existing classification systems.

Since *Diagnostic Classification: 0-3* is intended to complement existing approaches, readers should also refer to the *Diagnostic and Statistical Manual* of the American Psychiatric Association (DSM IV), which describes a number of mental health disorders usually first diagnosed in infancy, early childhood or adolescence. If a DSM IV diagnosis best describes the primary presenting difficulty, it should be coded under Axis I of this system. (For example, if the primary diagnosis is pica or rumination disorder, a diagnosis not listed in this system, then the DSM IV diagnosis should be listed under Axis I as the primary diagnosis.) If a DSM IV diagnosis is related to a primary diagnosis under this system, it should be listed under Axis III of this system.

Many medical disorders of infants and young children also involve a developmental difficulty. Such relevant medical conditions would be listed under Axis III of the current system; they are not to be treated as an alternative diagnosis, but as a co-existing problem. Appropriate classification frameworks such as the *International Classification of Diseases* (ICD 9 or ICD 10) should be used for this purpose. Similarly, educators, speech pathologists, occupational and physical therapists use classifications to organize and systematize developmental findings having to do with communication, motor and sensory functioning. These related diagnoses can be identified under Axis III of this classification system.

The reader will observe that some of the diagnostic categories that follow are described in more detail than others, and that some categories have subtypes while others do not. Familiar categories (similar to categories used with older children and adults) are generally described more briefly. Categories that are more specific to infancy and early childhood and/or based on more recent clinical experience or research are described in greater detail. Subtypes are presented for some categories in order to foster progress in research and clinical intervention planning. It should be reemphasized that this classification effort is a dynamic one, expected to change and grow with the field of clinical work with infants, young children and their families.

Guidelines to selecting the appropriate diagnosis

Some maladaptive behaviors observed in infants and young children are described in more than one of the various categories identified as primary disorders in Axis I. Because an infant or young child, in comparison with an adult, is capable of only a limited number of behavioral patterns or responses to various stresses or difficulties (e.g., somatic symptoms, irritability, withdrawal, impulsivity, fears, and developmental delays), some overlap is inevitable. The primary diagnosis should reflect the most prominent features of the disorder.

To facilitate deciding which diagnostic category should be of primary consideration for a given set of difficulties, the following guidelines may be useful. They will assist the clinician in determining which diagnosis takes precedence.

1. If there is a clear stress that is severe or significant enough, i.e. a specific overwhelming episode or multiple repeated trauma, associated with the disordered behavior or emotions, then traumatic stress disorder should be considered as a first option, i.e., the disorder would not be present without that stress.

2. If there is a clear constitutionally- or maturationally-based sensory, motor, processing, organizational, or integration difficulty which is associated with the observed maladaptive behavioral and/or emotional patterns, regardless of the particular symptoms, then regulatory disorders should be considered as a first option.

3. If the presenting problems are mild and of relatively short duration (less than four months), and associated with a clear environmental event, such as a parent's return to work, a move, or change in child care, then an adjustment disorder diagnosis should be considered.

4. Where there is neither a clear constitutionally- or maturationally-based vulnerability, nor a severe or significant stress or trauma, and when the difficulty is not mild, of short duration, and not associated with a clear event, then the categories of disorders of mood and affect should be considered.

5. Disorders of multiple delays, including communication and social relatedness, are extreme and distinct enough to be recognizable in their own right. They usually involve chronic patterns of maladaptation, as in the case of multisystem developmental disorders, and an ongoing rather than acute pattern of deprivation (in distinction from traumatic stress disorder), as in the case of reactive attachment deprivation/maltreatment disorder of infancy. These two disorders should take precedence over other categories such as

regulatory disorders or traumatic stress disorders. In other words, these two disorders are exceptions to the general rules listed above.

6. Where a particular difficulty occurs only in a certain situation or in relationship to a particular person, a diagnosis of adjustment disorder and relationship disorder should be considered. For example, a child is depressed, but only in the child care setting, or a child is very labile but only in the presence of a particular caregiver.

7. If the only difficulty involves the relationship and there are no other symptoms independent of that relationship, then do not use Axis I (Primary Classification) and use Axis II (Relationship Classification) to indicate the nature of the difficulty.

8. Reactive attachment deprivation/maltreatment disorder should be reserved for inadequate basic physical, psychological and emotional care. Concerns about the relationship or attachment can be reflected by the relationship axis or other diagnoses related to the specific symptom picture.

9. When such common symptoms such as feeding and sleep disorders are present, it is necessary to assess the underlying basis for these difficulties, which may be problems in their own right, or part of various diagnostic categories. For example, feeding or eating difficulties may follow an acute trauma, be a temporary reaction to a move or parent going to work (adaptation reaction), or related to physical problems. These difficulties may also be part of a more ongoing pattern as in reactive attachment disorder, or regulatory and multisystem developmental disorders.

   Sleep disorders, however, may be a distinct difficulty, as in the first year of life, without other presenting difficulties, or part of regulatory difficulties related to hypersensitivities and other sensory processing difficulties.

10. At times there will be a number of elements present which will make the diagnosis confusing. We may, for example, identify elements of acute stress or trauma, underlying constitutional vulnerabilities in sensory processing or motor planning capacities, together with disturbances of affect and mood and/or chronic patterns of withdrawal or avoidance (as seen in multisystem developmental disorders). In such complex situations, the diagnostician should try to make a judgment regarding the most prominent characteristics or contributing feature and follow the guidelines above.

11. On rare occasions, a child may have two primary conditions (e.g., a sleep disorder and a separation anxiety disorder). In such instances, one can list two primary diagnoses.

   The examples below illustrate the process of choosing a primary diagnosis.

   a. An infant with underlying over-sensitivity to touch and sound is developing adequately, but is traumatized by being close to a bombing or a fire (and the accompanying social disorganization). The infant then becomes withdrawn and frightened. A diagnosis under the category of psychic trauma disorder would be considered first, because the child's underlying constitutional vulnerability had not derailed his development until it interacted with a severe psychic trauma. The withdrawn behavior is secondary to the acute trauma.

b. A fearful and highly anxious infant startles every time she is touched by a stranger or hears an unexpected, loud noise close by. But when examined hands-on by a clinician who has taken the time to build rapport and a comfortable relationship, the child shows no clear evidence of sensory hyperreactivity or processing difficulties. In such a situation, it would appear that the seeming regulatory problems are actually secondary to the anxiety and/or fears. Therefore, anxiety disorders of infancy would be considered as first option.

c. A child with severe communication and relationship difficulties also evidences difficulties in sensory reactivity, sensory processing, and motor planning. Since both multisystem developmental disorders and regulatory disorders share constitutional and maturational variations, in this not unusual circumstance, the prominent behavioral features of the disturbance, such as difficulties with communication and social relatedness, would take precedence over the underlying constitutional contribution, i.e., multisystem developmental disorder over regulatory disorder.

Case vignettes at the end of the classification system will further discuss the reasoning processes involved in selecting a diagnosis.

Ongoing research efforts

This classification system presented in this volume is a **developing** system. It will be refined and updated periodically, based on systematic data collection and analysis and continuing discussion of cases.

Preliminary analyses of data already collected indicate that:

• the proposed new primary diagnostic categories do not significantly overlap with DSM IV;

• the new diagnostic categories take into account and differentiate the range of symptoms seen; and

• expert clinicians can reliably agree on primary diagnosis using the system proposed in *DC: 0-3*.

A clinical data collection form, with guidelines for its use, is available. This form is designed as a framework for use by experienced infant clinicians and trainees under supervision to organize the descriptive information and clinical impressions made during an assessment and to assure that the clinician completes a comprehensive assessment. To receive an electronic copy of the form and instructions, please contact Emily Fenichel via e-mail at e.fenichel@zerotothree.org.

Axis I Primary Diagnosis

The primary diagnosis should reflect the most prominent features of the disorder. Guidelines to selecting the appropriate diagnosis appear on pages 16-18.

100. Traumatic Stress Disorder

Traumatic Stress Disorder describes a continuum of symptoms which may be shown by children who have experienced a single event, a series of connected traumatic events, or chronic, enduring stress. These might include an infant or toddler's direct experience, witnessing, or confrontation with an event or events that involve actual or threatened death or serious injury to the child or others, or a threat to the psychological or physical integrity of the child or others. The traumatic event may be a sudden and unexpected event (e.g., earthquake, terrorist attack, mauling by an animal); a series of connected events (e.g., repeated air raids); or a chronic, enduring situation (e.g., chronic battering or sexual abuse).

The nature of the child's symptoms must be understood in the context of the trauma, the child's own personality characteristics, and his or her caregivers' ability to help the child cope, in terms of a sense of protection and safety, as well as working through the experience. In some cases, the memories children report may change as part of their attempts to rework the trauma. Thus change in a young child's account of the trauma does not necessarily indicate that the trauma was simply a fantasy.

Especially with severe trauma, like life-threatening injury to a family member, it is important to make the diagnosis and begin working with the child and family immediately. In most circumstances, without effective intervention, traumatic stress reactions will persist.

In making the diagnosis of traumatic stress disorder, the clinician should look for the existence of a traumatic event and the phenomena listed below:

1. A re-experiencing of the traumatic event(s) as evidenced by at least one of the following:

   a. Post-traumatic play — that is, play that represents a reenactment of some aspect of the trauma, is compulsively driven, fails to relieve anxiety, and is literal and less elaborate and imaginative than usual. This is seen instead of adaptive play reenactment — that is, play that represents some aspect of the trauma but lacks the other characteristics of post-traumatic play.

   Example: A toddler who was bitten by a dog plays out a scene in which she growls and snarls, then makes sudden lunges. She does not comment on this play, and repeats the scene with little variation. In contrast, an example of adaptive play reenactment might be a toddler who was bitten by a dog playing out numerous scenes of scary dogs, with different circumstances and outcomes apparent. The content of the play changes over time.

   b. Recurrent recollections of the traumatic event outside play — that is, repeated statements or questions about the event that suggest a fascination with the event or preoccupation with some aspect of the event. Distress is not necessarily apparent.

   Example: A toddler who was bitten by a dog talks endlessly about dogs and seems drawn to their images in books or on television.

   c. Repeated nightmares, especially if content can be ascertained and has obvious links to the trauma.

   d. Distress at exposure to reminders of the trauma.

   e. Episodes with objective features of a flashback or dissociation — that is, reenactment of the event without any sense of where the ideas for the reenactment are coming from, i.e., the behavior is dissociated from the child's intentionality or sense of purpose.

   Example: A toddler engaged in doll play does not comment on the sound of a siren in the street but abruptly begins a fighting sequence with the dolls, having been reminded of the ambulance which arrived after an argument between her parents.

2. A numbing of responsiveness in a child or interference with developmental momentum, appearing after a traumatic event and revealed by at least one of the following:

   a. Increased social withdrawal.

   b. Restricted range of affect.

   c. Temporary loss of previously acquired developmental skills, e.g., toilet training, language, relating to others.

   d. A decrease or constriction in play compared to the child's pattern before the traumatic event.

   Note: Constriction of play does not necessarily preclude post-traumatic play or play reenactment.

3. Symptoms of increased arousal that appear after a traumatic event, as revealed by at least one of the following:

a. Night terrors — that is, symptoms of an arousal disorder in which the child starts from sleep with a panicky scream, has agitated motor movements, is unresponsive and inconsolable, and shows signs of autonomic arousal, such as rapid breathing, racing pulse, and sweating. The episodes tend to occur in the first third of the night and last from one to five minutes. No content can be ascertained at the time or the following day.

b. Difficulty going to sleep, evidenced by strong bedtime protest or trouble falling asleep.

c. Repeated night waking unrelated to nightmares or night terrors.

d. Significant attentional difficulties and decreased concentration.

e. Hypervigilance.

f. Exaggerated startle response.

4. Symptoms, especially fears or aggression, that were not present before the traumatic event, including at least one of the following:

a. Aggression toward peers, adults or animals.

b. Separation anxiety.

c. Fear of toileting alone.

d. Fear of the dark.

e. Other new fears.

f. Pessimism or self-defeating behavior, manipulativeness (designed to gain control), or masochistic provocativeness (behavior that provokes abuse).

g. Sexual and aggressive behaviors inappropriate for a child's age.

h. Other nonverbal reactions experienced at the time of the trauma, including somatic symptoms, motor reenactments, skin stigmata, pain, or posturing.

i. Other new symptoms.

If a traumatic event has occurred and symptoms listed above are present, the diagnosis of Traumatic Stress Disorder takes precedence over other primary diagnoses.

200. Disorders of Affect

This group of disorders is related to the infant or young child's affective experience and behavioral expressiveness. Included in the group are anxiety disorders, mood disorders, a mixed disorder of emotional expressiveness, childhood gender identity disorder, and reactive attachment disorder. This category focuses on the infant's experience and on symptoms which are a general feature of the child's functioning rather than specific to a situation or relationship.

Young children with affect disorders do not manifest severe developmental delays or significant constitutional or maturational variations. Thus, the affect disorders may be contrasted with regulatory or multisystem developmental disorders: regulatory disorders have a clear constitutional or maturational contribution, and multisystem disorders involve multiple developmental difficulties.

Affect disorders are often associated with certain relationship or interactive patterns between child and caregiver. (Specific patterns are identified under Relationship Disorders [Axis II]. These diagnoses should be used when these relationship or interactive patterns dominate and characterize the primary caregiver's relationship with the infant or young child.) To qualify as a disorder of affect, however, interactive difficulties, even when in part due to a particular relationship or context, must not be evident **only** in a single relationship or context, but must be associated with general affective and behavioral difficulties **in the child**.

Therefore, when considering disorders of affect, the clinician must determine whether the symptoms are a **general** feature of the child's functioning or **specific** to a situation or relationship. It is important to remember that relationship or interaction patterns are seldom one-dimensional. Parents, other caregivers and infants interact and relate in many complex ways at different times. An otherwise competent caregiver may be unable to deal with selected infant or child behaviors or temperamental inclinations — for example, an infant's assertiveness, dependency, or excitability. Parent/child relationships may encounter difficulties at certain stages of development which involve negotiating particular needs or developmental challenges. In some infant/caregiver relationships, however, patterns which do not support the infant's emotional development may become more predominant. These patterns may include adult over- or under-protectiveness, over- or under-stimulation, poor synchrony, misreading or misperception of infant's or child's cues or functional emotional developmental level, lack of empathy, avoidant or indiscriminate patterns, etc. When these patterns persist, they may begin to affect the child's functioning even when he or she is not interacting in that particular relationship. The diagnosis of affect disorder may apply when a problem (such as fearfulness), while originally characteristic of a specific relationship, nonetheless affects the child's functioning in other areas and with other people.

201. Anxiety Disorders of Infancy and Early Childhood

A diagnosis of anxiety disorder should be based upon evidence of an infant or toddler's excessive levels of anxiety or fear, beyond expectable reactions to normal developmental challenges and manifested by any one of the following:

1. Multiple or specific fears.

2. Excessive separation anxiety or stranger anxiety.

3. Episodes of excessive anxiety or panic without clear precipitant.

4. Excessive inhibition or constriction of behavior due to anxiety (when there is severe constriction without identifiable anxiety, consider Mixed Disorder of Emotional Expressiveness [204], described below) .

5. Severe anxiety, associated with a lack of development of basic ego functions ordinarily expected to emerge between ages 2 - 4. These functions include impulse control, increasingly stable mood regulation, reality testing, and emergence of a cohesive sense of self.

6. Agitation in the infant, uncontrollable crying or screaming, sleeping and eating disturbances, recklessness, and other behavioral manifestations of anxiety.

To qualify as a disorder, the anxiety or fear should persist for at least two weeks and interfere with appropriate functioning (e.g., social relationships, play, speech, sleep, eating, etc.).

In considering a diagnosis of Anxiety Disorder, the clinician should view presenting symptoms, their duration, and their degree of interference with functioning in relation to the child's developmental level. For example, a child with cognitive delay who is at the developmental age of expectable stranger anxiety would *not* meet criterion. A child with developmental delays *can* be diagnosed as exhibiting an anxiety disorder if the anxiety/fear is inappropriate to his or her developmental level.

In making a diagnosis of Anxiety Disorder, the clinician should keep the following guidelines in mind.

• When known trauma(s) are evident and the onset of the child's difficulties follow the trauma, then Traumatic Stress Disorder would take precedence.

• Anxiety disorders should not be diagnosed in the presence of Multisystem Developmental Disorder (MSDD). The MSDD would take precedence.

• If there are clear sensory reactivity, receptive language and auditory processing, visual-spatial processing, or motor planning difficulties, regulatory disorders would take precedence.

• If the child's anxiety or fear is limited to a particular relationship, then a Relationship Disorder only should be considered.

202. Mood Disorder: Prolonged Bereavement/Grief Reaction

This category is based on the premise that the loss of a primary caregiver such as a parent is almost always a serious problem for an infant or young child because most young children do not have the emotional and cognitive resources to deal with such a major loss. Moreover, a child who is grieving may have an "other" critical caregiver who is also grieving, and consequently not available for support. The child's grieving may then be compounded. Every effort should be made to support the physical and emotional availability of other caregivers to the grieving infant or young child. All grief reactions require close monitoring and intervention even when symptoms are transient.

Manifestations of this condition can include any stage of the sequence of protest, despair, and detachment. Symptoms could include the following:

1. The child may cry, call, and search for the absent parent, refusing the attempts of others to provide comfort.

2. Emotional withdrawal may be present, with lethargy, sad facial expression, and lack of interest in age-appropriate activities.

3. Eating and sleeping may be disrupted.

4. There may be regression or loss of previously achieved developmental milestones — for example, a child may revert to bed wetting or baby talk.

5. The child may show constricted range of affect..

6. Detachment may appear. This may take the form of seeming indifference toward reminders of the caregiver figure, such as a photograph or mention of his or her name, or selective "forgetting," with apparent lack of recognition of these reminders.

7. Alternatively, the child may become extremely sensitive to any reminder of the caregiver, showing acute distress when a possession that belonged to the caregiver is touched by another or taken away. Such possessions or reminders may be sources of comfort and happy recollections, since the young child is not yet cognizant of the permanence of the loss. A child may also react with strong emotion to any theme remotely connected with separation and loss, refusing, for example, to play hide-and-seek or bursting into tears when a household object is moved from its customary place.

This disorder may not be easy to distinguish from Traumatic Stress Disorder. The clinician needs to pay attention to the nature of the symptoms. In Traumatic Stress Disorder, there is a greater tendency towards anxious reenactment and compulsive patterns. In Prolonged Bereavement/Grief Reaction there is a greater tendency for depression and apathy.

203. Mood Disorder: Depression of Infancy and Early Childhood

This category is reserved for infants and young children who exhibit a pattern of depressed or irritable mood with diminished interest and/or pleasure in developmentally appropriate activities, diminished capacity to protest, excessive whining, and a diminished repertoire of social interactions and initiative. These symptoms may be accompanied by disturbances in sleep or eating, including weight loss.

The symptoms must be present for a period of at least two weeks.

When this disorder is observed in the presence of significant psychosocial/environmental deprivation, this should be noted and Reactive Attachment Deprivation/Maltreatment Disorder of Infancy should be considered as an alternative classification, especially if the deprivation is severe. If the disorder is not severe and is observed in the context of an adjustment which the child is in the process of making (for example, to a parent's return to work), then Adjustment Disorder should be considered. When neither of these patterns is present then Depression should be considered as the primary disorder.

204. Mixed Disorder of Emotional Expressiveness

This category should be used for infants and young children who have an ongoing difficulty expressing developmentally appropriate emotions. Their difficulties are understood as reflecting problems in their affective development and experiences. The disorder may be manifested by:

1. The absence or near absence of one or more specific types of affects that are developmentally expectable — for example, pleasure, displeasure, joy, anger, fear, curiosity, shame, sadness, excitement, envy, jealousy, empathy, pride, etc. Included here is the absence of fears, concerns, or anxieties that are expected at certain stages of development and serve adaptive or protective goals — for example, affects which serve as *signal* anxiety to separation or body damage fears. It is important to remember that some children experience these expected fears and anxieties but do not express them directly; rather, they may appear overly aggressive, reckless, or overly independent.

2. A range of emotional expression that is constricted in comparison to developmentally appropriate expectations. Marked affective inhibition or reduced affective range may be observed. Sometimes diminished affect will be mostly evidenced through a diminished range of expected behaviors. For example, a child with persistent and massive avoidance may lack the capacity to

be assertive and explorative, or a child who is persistently negativistic and oppositional may be unable to cooperate and collaborate.

3. Disturbed intensity of emotional expression, inappropriate to the child's developmental level — for example, either excessive intensity, usually accompanied by poor modulation of affective expression, or blandness and apathy.

4. Reversal of affect or affect inappropriate to situations — for example, laughing when upset.

This diagnosis should not be used if the child is given a diagnosis of anxiety or depression. This diagnosis should be used with children with developmental delays only if the disturbance in affective expression is inappropriate to the child's developmental level.

205. Childhood Gender Identity Disorder

Childhood Gender Identity Disorder (GID) entails a circumscribed disturbance in the experience of the child's own gender which becomes manifest during the sensitive period of gender identity development (between approximately 2-4 years) when the child first learns to classify self and others by gender. Children with gender identity disorder have a profound and pervasive sense of discomfort, anxiety, and/or sense of inappropriateness connected to their own gender. The discomfort with their own gender is matched by an equally intense wish to be the opposite gender, which will be manifest in play, fantasy, and choice of activities, peers, and clothing according to the developmental level of the child's understanding of gender stereotypes.

The criteria below are consistent with those described in DSM IV and appear here because GID is a new category in both systems. The following description of this disorder includes a more detailed description of the types of behaviors and attitudes seen in very young children with this kind of challenge. The criteria include:

1. A strong and persistent cross-gender identification (not merely a desire for any perceived cultural advantages of being the opposite sex) as manifested by at least four of the following:

   a. Repeatedly stated desire to be, or insistence that he or she is the opposite sex.

   b. In boys, preference for cross-dressing or simulating female attire; in girls, insistence on wearing stereotypical masculine clothing.

   c. Strong and persistent preferences for cross-sex roles in fantasy play or persistent fantasies of being the opposite sex.

   d. Intense desire to participate in the games and pastimes of the opposite sex.

   e. Strong preference for playmates of the opposite sex.

2. Persistent discomfort with one's assigned sex or sense of inappropriateness in that gender role, manifested by any of the following:

a. In boys, assertion that the penis or testes are disgusting or will disappear or assertion that it would be better not to have a penis, or marked aversion toward male stereotypical toys, games, and activities, tied to the idea that he does not want to be a boy.

b. In girls, rejection of urination in a sitting position or assertion that she does not want to grow breasts or menstruate, or marked aversion toward normative feminine clothing, tied to the idea that she doesn't want to be a girl.

3. Absence of nonpsychiatric medical condition — for example, hermaphroditism.

The acquisition of the sense of one's own gender is a developmental process that affords much normal variation. It is essential to differentiate GID from the following normative variations as well as from other disorders that may appear to be similar.

1. **Normal Developmental Variability**
It is not uncommon for 2-3-year-old children to dress up and make believe that they are the other gender. This ordinarily will be manifested by children flexibly imitating mommy, daddy, sister, brother, the baby, or even the family pet. If the child is compulsively interested in cross-gender pretend play, and this continues, this pattern is very atypical, even at age 2.

2. **Gender Non-Conformity**
Children who have a well-established and positive sense of their own gender identity may also have cross-gender interests. A little boy may take up an interest in cooking, in growing flowers, in play-acting or in music and may not enjoy rough-and-tumble play. A little girl may discover that she is a better athlete than most of the boys her age, and begin to enjoy exercising her skills accordingly. This kind of behavior constitutes gender non-conformity and is not accompanied by a dislike of one's gender. It is not a pathological phenomenon and indeed may be associated with a greater degree of behavioral flexibility and health.

3. **Tomboyism**
GID in girls must be differentiated from tomboyism. Girls who prefer wearing pants, who enjoy rough-and-tumble play, and who prefer boys as playmates may be referred to as "tomboys." These girls are not distressed about being female and in fact may evidence a great deal of flexibility. In contrast, girls who exhibit these behaviors in the context of persistent distress about their gender, about their sexual anatomy, and/or about having to wear female clothing on any and all occasions are likely to have gender identity problems.

4. **The Wish To Be Both Genders**
Prior to the age of roughly 2 1/2 to 3 1/2, when children learn to categorize correctly by gender, many children experience themselves as able to do and

be all things, male and female. Thus, little boys may believe that they can give birth, little girls that they may grow a penis while yet remaining girls. Giving up this illusion involves a loss. Some toddlers whose feeling of self-worth is especially brittle may have trouble negotiating this period and will show signs in their behavior that they still strongly harbor some of the old hopes of being both genders, and express rage and envy at whichever parent or sibling seems to them to have dashed their hopes. This is not GID — in GID, the child wants to be *one* gender — the opposite one — not both.

5. Children with Intersex Conditions
True intersex conditions include hypospadias or a micro-phallus in boys or an enlarged clitoris in girls. These conditions may give rise to confusion about gender but rarely to GID.

The circumscribed disturbance in the area of gender is striking in its *pervasiveness, persistence, and duration.* Its diagnosis can be made reliably through observation, parental report, psychological assessment or interviewing, depending on the age and accessibility of the child. In very young boys, beginning at about age $1^1/_2$ to 2, the wish to be a girl may be expressed verbally or indirectly in persistent fantasy enactments such as cross-dressing in play. Boys with GID often dress up in their mother's or sister's clothes; where dresses are unavailable, they may improvise with towels, T-shirts, blankets, or scarves. The boy will rigidly enact feminine roles in play, and his favorite stories and videotapes will involve female figures such as the Little Mermaid, Cinderella, and Snow White. Boys with GID will often spend hours playing with Barbie dolls. Similarly, the boy may show an intense fascination with jewelry, cosmetics, high-heeled shoes, nail polish, etc. As these boys get older, and begin to understand that genitals are the emblem of gender, many will say that they dislike their penis or that they want a vagina. Some refuse to urinate standing up. It has been reported that some boys with extreme GID may attempt to cut their penises off.

Girls with GID intensely dislike being girls and wish to be boys. They are physically active, athletic, and have a marked preference for boys as playmates. They not only typically refuse to wear dresses, preferring only pants, but will become enraged and panicked if required to wear a dress for a special occasion. Many insist that their mothers buy them clothes only from the boys' department of a store. Most cut their hair short; many adopt a gender-neutral nickname and insist on using the boys' bathroom in public places. Rejection of urination in a sitting position is common in girls with GID, as is the assertion that a girl has or wants to grow a penis and, conversely, does not want ever to have to babies.

Boys with GID usually have a shy, inhibited temperament, which is particularly evident in transitions and new situations. They typically avoid rough-and-tumble play and are usually less physically active than other boys their age. Many have remarkable imitative capacities that make them particularly skilled at play-acting. They are very often talented in the visual arts and music. The majority of the boys have heightened sensory reactivity to odor and to colors; a subgroup has similar reactivity to texture and sound. Not only do these boys appear more alive to the sensory world, but they are also more vulnerable to it.

Far less is known about the constitutional predisposition of girls with GID. They appear to be bolder and more active than other girls. Unlike boys with GID, they are highly invested in athletic activities. Despite their more extroverted nature, our clinical impression is that these girls have as high an anxiety level as boys but manage their anxiety with different defensive strategies.

Boys especially experience separation anxiety disorder, most are fearful of bodily injury, and a majority have symptoms of depression. About two-thirds are insecurely attached.

It has recently been found that girls, like boys with GID, have as many symptoms of behavioral disturbance as do other children who are referred to psychiatric clinics for help.

Most observers of this disorder have noted that once the disorder is set in motion, the parents of children with GID do not discourage the cross-gender behavior.

The histories of boys with GID regularly reveal significant traumas in the family during the first three years of life or chronic severe marital stress. A history of maternal depression and anxiety and paternal substance abuse, anxiety, or depression is present in the vast majority of cases. During the sensitive period for the child's development of an understanding of gender (between the ages of 2-4 years), mothers typically have been depressed in reaction to an event that they experienced as traumatic, in a family context in which the father was emotionally unavailable.

In girls as well as boys, a history of significant trauma in the family and/or chronic severe marital stress during the child's first three years of life is regularly found.

206. Reactive Attachment Deprivation/Maltreatment Disorder of Infancy

This disorder is observed in the context of evidence of deprivation or maltreatment, manifested in any of the following ways:

1. Persistent parental neglect or abuse of a physical or psychological nature, of sufficient intensity and duration to undermine the child's basic sense of security and attachment;

2. Frequent changes in, or the inconsistent availability of, the primary caregiver, making an attachment to an individual caregiver impossible; or

3. Other environmental compromises and situations beyond the control of the

parent and child which are prolonged, interfere with the appropriate care of the child, and prevent stable attachments.

Without the presence of strong protective factors (i.e., almost daily visits by parents, the daily involvement of an individual nurse or aide), infants and young children are likely to be deprived of emotionally and developmentally appropriate care in long-term hospitalization, when they experience multiple or changing caregivers, or when parents are depressed or involved in substance abuse. The child with reactive attachment disorder will usually fail to initiate social interactions or will manifest ambivalent or contradictory social responses — for example, approach-avoidance responses to caregivers or others, or extreme vigilance, or excessively inhibited or apathetic responses to social interactions. A child may also show developmentally inappropriate social relatedness by social indiscriminateness — for example, excessive sociability with relative strangers. Not all children who have been neglected or abused will exhibit this disorder. Usually some remission of the symptoms will follow amelioration of the caregiving environment.

This disorder is very similar to Reactive Attachment Disorder of Infancy or Early Childhood, as described in DSM IV.

Before making this diagnosis, the clinician should consider other related diagnoses. Some caregiving difficulties that affect the child — for example, overprotectiveness or anxiety on the part of the caregiver — are best described by one of the primary affect or relationship classifications that are concerned with the quality and interactive nature of the infant/caregiver relationship. If the conditions interfering with the maintenance of the relationship are temporary or reactive to severe stress, consider adjustment reaction, psychic trauma disorder, or the relationship disorders.

The disorder may be associated with failure to thrive or other growth disturbance (which should also be coded separately under Axis III). The condition is difficult to diagnose in the presence of severe or profound retardation or multisystem developmental disorder. The diagnostic profile of a child with Deprivation/Maltreatment Disorder will be enriched by the information coded under Axis II, Relationship Disorders.

300. Adjustment Disorder

The diagnosis of adjustment disorder should be considered for mild, transient situational disturbances which cannot be explained by or meet the criteria of the other proposed diagnoses. The onset of the difficulties must be tied to a clear environmental event or change, such as the mother's return to work, a family move, a change in day care, or illness. As a result of the child's developmental age, unique constitutional characteristics, and family circumstances, the infant or toddler experiences a temporary reaction, lasting days

or weeks but no longer than four months. To make this diagnosis, the clinician should be able to identify both the clear environmental event and the
transient nature of the symptoms.

The child may present affective symptoms (for example, the child is subdued, sober or withdrawn), or behavioral symptoms (for example, the child
is oppositional, resists going to sleep, has frequent tantrums, or regresses in
toilet training).

The description of this disorder is consistent with that in DSM IV but
has been described here in terms more sensitive and relevant to infants and
young children. The time frame of four months reflects the relatively short
life span of the child under three or four years of age.

Both the clear environmental event and the transient nature of the symptoms are essential for this classification. This diagnosis should not be used
when symptoms are due to ongoing family patterns or the ongoing interplay
between constitutional and motor patterns and family patterns, or when
there is a severe trauma. In these instances the disorders of anxiety, mood and
relationship disorders, regulatory disorders or traumatic stress disorder
should be considered.

400. Regulatory Disorders

Regulatory disorders are first evident in infancy and early childhood. They
are characterized by the infant or young child's difficulties in regulating
behavior and physiological, sensory, attentional, motor or affective processes, and in organizing a calm, alert, or affectively positive state. The classification suggested below includes four types of regulatory disorders. The oper-
ational definition for each type includes a distinct behavioral pattern, **coupled with** a sensory, sensory-motor, or organizational processing difficulty
which affects the child's daily adaptation and interaction/relationships.

Poorly organized or modulated responses may show themselves in the following domains:

1. The physiological or state repertoire (e.g., irregular breathing, startles, hic-
cups, gagging).

2. Gross motor activity (e.g., motor disorganization, jerky movements, constant movement).

3. Fine motor activity (e.g., poorly differentiated or sparse, jerky, or limp movements).

4. Attentional organization (e.g., "driven" behavior, inability to settle down, or,
conversely, perseveration about a small detail).

5. Affective organization, including the predominant affective tone (e.g., sober,
depressed, or happy); the range of affect (e.g., broad or constricted); and the

degree of modulation expressed (e.g., infant shifts abruptly from being completely calm to screaming frantically) and the capacity to use and organize affect as part of relationships and interaction with others (e.g., avoidant, negativistic, clinging and demanding behavior patterns).

6. Behavioral organization (e.g., aggressive or impulsive behavior).

7. Sleep, eating, or elimination patterns.

8. Language (receptive and expressive) and cognitive difficulties.

Presenting problems in the behavior of infants and young children may include sleep or feeding difficulties, behavior control difficulties, fearfulness and anxiety, difficulties in speech and language development, and impaired ability to play alone or with others. Parents may also complain that a child gets upset easily or loses his temper and has difficulty adapting to changes. (Because the daily routines of caregiving involve continuous sensory, motor, and affective experiences for the infant and young child, handling that is not sensitive to individual differences, irregular conditions in the environment, and/or changes in routine can strongly affect infants and children with regulatory disorders as well as their caregivers.)

Many attentional, affective motor, sensory, behavioral control, and language problems that have traditionally been viewed as difficulties in their own right may in certain children be part of a larger regulatory disorder. Clinicians have used general terms such as "overly sensitive," "difficult temperament," or "reactive" to describe sensory, motor, and integrative patterns that are presumed to be "constitutionally" or "biologically" based, but without delineating specifically the sensory pathway or motor functions involved. There is growing evidence that constitutional and early maturational patterns contribute to the difficulties of such infants, but it is also recognized that early caregiving patterns can exert considerable influence on how constitutional and maturational patterns develop and become part of the child's evolving personality. As interest in these children increases, it is important to systematize descriptions of the sensory, motor, and integrative patterns presumed to be involved.

The diagnosis of regulatory disorder involves **both** a distinct behavioral pattern **and** a sensory, sensory-motor, or organizational processing difficulty. When both features are not present, other diagnoses may be more appropriate. For example, an infant who is irritable and withdrawn after being abandoned may be evidencing an expectable type of relationship or attachment difficulty. An infant who is irritable and overly reactive to routine interpersonal experiences, in the absence of a clearly identified sensory, sensory-motor, or processing difficulty, may be evidencing an anxiety or mood disorder. (Sleep or eating difficulties can be symptoms of a regulatory disorder, or be part of separate diagnostic categories.)

To make the diagnosis of regulatory disorder in an infant or young child, the clinician should observe **both** a sensory, sensory-motor, or processing difficulty from the list below, and one or more behavioral symptoms.

1. Over- or under-reactivity to loud or high- or low-pitched noises.

2. Over- or under-reactivity to bright lights or new and striking visual images, such as colors, shapes, and complex fields.

3. Tactile defensiveness (e.g., over-reactivity to dressing; bathing; stroking of arms, legs, or trunk; avoidance of touching "messy" textures) and/or oral hypersensitivity (e.g., avoidance of food with certain textures).

4. Oral-motor difficulties or incoordination influenced by poor muscle tone, motor planning difficulties, and/or oral tactile hypersensitivity (e.g., avoids certain food textures).

5. Under-reactivity to touch or pain.

6. Gravitational insecurity — that is, under- or over-reactivity in a child with normal postural responses (e.g., balance reactions) to the changing sensations of movement involved in brisk horizontal or vertical movements (e.g., being tossed in the air, playing merry-go-round, or jumping).

7. Under- or over-reactivity to odors.

8. Under- or over-reactivity to temperature.

9. Poor muscle tone and muscle stability — e.g., hypotonia, hypertonia, postural fixation, or lack of smooth movement quality.

10. Qualitative deficits in motor planning skills (e.g., difficulty in sequencing the hand movements necessary to explore a novel or complex toy or difficulty climbing a jungle gym).

11. Qualitative deficits in ability to modulate motor activity (not secondary to anxiety or interactive difficulties).

12. Qualitative deficits in fine motor skills.

13. Qualitative deficits in articulation capacity (e.g., for an 8-month-old, difficult imitating distinct sounds; for 3-year-old, difficulty finding words to describe an intended or completed action).

14. Qualitative deficits in visual-spatial processing capacities (e.g., for an 8-month-old, difficulty in recognizing different facial configurations; for a 2-1/2-year-old, difficulty in knowing in which direction to turn to get to another room in a familiar house; for a 3-1/2 year old, difficulty in using visual-spatial cues to recognize and categorize different shapes).

15. Qualitative deficits in capacity to attend and focus, not related to anxiety, interactive difficulties, or clear auditory/verbal or visual/spatial processing problems.

Types of Regulatory Disorders

The four types of regulatory disorders described below are based on the predominant characteristics of the child, including behavioral patterns and emotional inclinations, as well as motor and sensory patterns. The first three subtypes are to be used to subclassify the disorder where a tendency towards one predominant pattern is observable. Because some children will not be adequately described by these subtypes, there is an "other" subtype. Note that the description of the first three subtypes includes a discussion of caregiving patterns which promote better regulation and organization in the child, as well as caregiving patterns that intensify the child's difficulty.

401. Type I: Hypersensitive

Infants and young children who are over-reactive or hypersensitive to various stimuli show a range of behavioral patterns. Two patterns are characteristic, (1) fearful and cautious, and (2) negative and defiant. In addition, children may be inconsistent in their hypersensitivity. Sensitivities may also vary throughout the day. Most often sensory input tends to have a cumulative effect, so that a child may not be bothered by initial input, but have significant difficulty at the end of the day. In addition, response to sensory input seems to interact with the baseline level of arousal. If the child is stressed or tired, less sensory input may be required to trigger a hypersensitive response.

Fearful and Cautious:

Behavioral patterns include excessive cautiousness, inhibition and/or fearfulness. In early infancy, these patterns are manifested by a restricted range of exploration and assertiveness, dislike of changes in routine, and a tendency to be frightened and clinging in new situations. Young children's behavior is characterized by excessive fears and/or worries and by shyness in new experiences, such as forming peer relationships or engaging with new adults. The child may have a fragmented, rather than an integrated, internal representational world, and may be easily distracted by different stimuli. Occasionally, the child behaves impulsively when overloaded and/or frightened. The child tends to be easily upset (e.g., irritable, often crying), cannot soothe himself readily (e.g., finds it difficult to return to sleep), and cannot quickly recover from frustration or disappointment.

Motor and sensory patterns are characterized by over-reactivity to touch, loud noises, or bright lights. The child often has adequate auditory-verbal processing abilities but compromised visual-spatial processing ability. The child may also be overreactive to movement in space and have motor planning challenges.

Caregiver patterns which enhance flexibility and assertiveness in fearful and cautious children involve empathy, especially for the child's sensory and affective experience; very gradual and supportive encouragement to explore new experiences; and gentle, but firm, limits. Inconsistent caregiver patterns intensify these children's difficulties, as when caregivers are overindulgent and/or overprotective some of the time and punitive and/or intrusive at other times.

Negative and Defiant:

Behavioral patterns are negativistic, stubborn, controlling, and defiant. The child often does the opposite of what is requested or expected. The child has difficulty in making transitions, and prefers repetition, absence of change, or, at most, change at a slow pace. Infants tend to be fussy, difficult, and resistant to transitions and changes. Preschoolers tend to be negative, angry, defiant and stubborn, as well as compulsive and perfectionistic. However, these children can evidence joyful, flexible behavior at certain times.

In contrast to the fearful/cautious or avoidant child, the negative and defiant child does not become fragmented but organizes an integrated sense of self around negative, defiant patterns. In contrast to the impulsive, stimulus-seeking child (Type III, below) the negative and defiant child is more controlling, tending to avoid or be slow to engage in new experiences, rather than to crave them, and is not generally aggressive unless provoked.

Motor and sensory patterns include a tendency toward over-reactivity to touch, which may be observed during play as the avoidance of certain textures or manipulation of materials with fingertips. Children with this pattern are also often over-reactive to sound. Children with this pattern often show intact or even precocious visual-spatial capacities, but their auditory processing capacity may be compromised. Children may have good muscle tone and postural control, but may show some difficulty in fine motor coordination and/or motor planning.

Caregiver patterns which enhance flexibility involve soothing, empathic support of slow, gradual change and avoidance of power struggles. Caregivers' warmth, even in the face of the child's negativism or rejection, and encouragement of symbolic representation of different affects, especially dependency, anger, and annoyance, also enhances flexibility. In contrast, caregiver patterns that are intrusive, excessively demanding, overstimulating, or punitive tend to intensify children's negative and defiant patterns.

402. TYPE II: Under-reactive

Infants and young children who are under-reactive to various stimuli may show one of two characteristic patterns: withdrawn and difficult to engage or self-absorbed, seeming to "march to the beat of their own drummer."

Withdrawn and Difficult to Engage:

Behavioral patterns of the withdrawn/difficult-to-engage child include seeming disinterest in exploring relationships or even challenging games or objects. Children may appear apathetic, easily exhausted, and withdrawn. High affective tone and saliency are required to attract their interest, attention, and emotional engagement. Infants may appear delayed or depressed, lacking in motor exploration and responsivity to sensations and social overtures. In addition to continuing the above patterns, preschoolers evidence diminished verbal dialogue. Their behavior and play may only present a limited range of ideas and fantasies. Sometimes children will seek out desired sensory input, often engaging in repetitive sensory activities, such as spinning on a sit-n-spin, swinging, or jumping up and down on the bed. The intensity or repetition of these activities is used to fully experience them.

Motor and sensory patterns are characterized by under-reactivity to sounds and movement in space, but either over- or under-reactivity to touch. Children with this pattern may have intact visual-spatial processing capacities, but often experience auditory-verbal processing difficulties. Poor motor quality and motor planning can often be observed as well as limited exploratory activity or flexibility in play.

Caregiver patterns that provide intense interactive input and foster initiative tend to help underreactive withdrawn children engage, attend, interact, and explore their environment. These patterns involve reaching out, energized wooing, and robust responses to the child's cues, however faint. In contrast, caregiver patterns that are low-key, "laid back," or depressive in tone and rhythm tend to intensify these children's patterns of withdrawal.

Self-Absorbed:

Behavioral patterns of self-absorbed children include creativity and imagination, combined with a tendency for the child to tune into his or her own sensations, thoughts, and emotions, rather than being tuned into and attentive to communications from other people. Infants may appear self-absorbed, becoming interested in objects through solitary exploration rather than in the context of interaction. Children may appear inattentive, easily distracted, or preoccupied, especially when not pulled into a task or interaction. Preschoolers tend to escape into fantasy in the presence of external challenges, such as competition with a peer or a demanding preschool activity. They may prefer to play by themselves when others do not actively join their fantasies. Within their fantasy life, these children may show enormous imagination and creativity.

Motor and sensory patterns include a tendency toward decreased auditory-verbal processing capacities coupled with an ability to create a rich range of ideas (receptive language difficulties, coupled with creativity and imagination, make it easier for a child to tune into his or her own ideas than to attend to another person's ideas). Children may or may not show irregularities in other sensory and motor capacities.

Caregiver patterns that are helpful include the tendency to tune into the child's nonverbal and verbal communications and help the child engage in two-way communication, i.e., "open and close circles of communication." Helpful caregiver patterns also encourage a good balance between fantasy and reality, and help a child who is attempting to escape into fantasy stay grounded in external reality, e.g., show sensitivity to the child's interests and feelings, promote discussion of daily events and feelings and make fantasy play a parent-child collaborative endeavor rather than a solitary child activity. In contrast, a caregiver's self-absorption or preoccupation or confusing family communications tend to intensify children's difficulties.

403. Type III: Motorically Disorganized, Impulsive

Children with this pattern evidence poor control of behavior coupled with craving sensory input. Some children appear aggressive and fearless. Others simply appear impulsive and disorganized.

Behavioral patterns among motorically disorganized children involve high activity, with children seeking contact and stimulation through deep pressure. The child appears to lack caution. Not infrequently, the motorically disorganized child's tendency to seek contact with people or objects leads to breaking things, intruding into other people's body spaces, unprovoked hitting, etc. Behavior that begins as a result of poor motor planning and organization may be interpreted by others as aggression rather than excitability. Once others react aggressively to the child, the child's own behavior may become aggressive in intent.

Motorically disorganized infants seek or crave sensory input and stimulation. Preschoolers often show excitable, aggressive, intrusive behavior and a daredevil, risk-taking style, as well as preoccupation with aggressive themes in pretend play. When the young child is anxious or unsure of himself, he may use counterphobic behaviors — for example, hitting before (possibly) getting hit or repeating unacceptable behavior after being asked to stop. When older and able to verbalize and self-observe his own patterns, the child may describe the need for activity and stimulation as a way to feel alive, vibrant and powerful.

Motor and sensory patterns are characterized by sensory under-reactivity, craving of sensory input, and motor discharge. The motorically disorganized child often combines under-reactivity to touch and sound, stimulus craving, and poor motor modulation and motor planning, and evidences diffuse, impulsive behavior towards persons and objects. Similarly, motor activities are unfocused and diffused. Due to his under-reactivity, the child may listen fleetingly, attend poorly, and yet crave loud noises or intense music. The craving of stimuli sometimes leads to destructive behavior. These children may evidence either auditory or visual-spatial processing difficulties, but may also evidence age appropriate patterns in these areas.

Caregiver patterns characterized by continuous, warm relating, a great deal of nurturance, and empathy, coupled with clear structure and limits, will enhance flexibility and adaptivity. It is helpful for caregivers to provide children with constructive opportunities for sensory and affective involvement, while encouraging modulation and self-regulation. Caregiver patterns that encourage the use of imagination in support of exploration of the external environment will further enhance the child's flexibility. In contrast, caregiver patterns that avoid warm continuous engagement, (e.g., changing caregivers) are overly punitive, fail to set clear limits and boundaries on behavior, and either over- or under-stimulate the child may intensify these difficulties.

404. Type IV: Other

This category should be used for children who meet the first criterion for regulatory disorder (i.e., motor or sensory processing difficulty) but whose behavioral patterns are not adequately described by one of the three subtypes above.

500. Sleep Behavior Disorder

The diagnosis of sleep disorder should be considered when a sleep disturbance is the only presenting problem in an infant or toddler under three years of age who has no accompanying sensory reactivity or sensory processing difficulties.

Sleep problems in infants are subdivided into disorders of initiating (e.g. settling into sleep) and maintaining sleep (e.g. waking up during the night, with difficulty returning to sleep). Infants may also show excessive somnolence, dysfunctions associated with sleep stage or arousal (e.g. night terrors) or difficulties in developing predictable sleep-wake schedules. Infants who have difficulty in initiating or maintaining sleep may also have problems in calming themselves and dealing with transitions from one stage of arousal to another.

This diagnosis should **not** be used when a young child's sleep problem is primarily due to anxiety, relationship or motor disturbance, transient adjustment problems, traumatic stress disorder, or any of the types of regulatory disorders noted above.

600. Eating Behavior Disorder

The diagnosis of eating behavior disorder, which may become evident at different stages of infancy and early childhood, should be considered when an infant or young child shows difficulties in establishing regular feeding patterns with adequate or appropriate food intake (e.g., nonorganic failure to thrive). The child does not regulate his or her eating in accordance with physiologic feelings of hunger or fullness. In the absence of general regulatory difficulties, interpersonal precipitants such as separation, negativism, trauma, etc., one should consider a primary eating disorder.

Specific feeding disorders of infancy and early childhood such as pica and rumination can be found in DSM IV.

This category should not be used as a primary diagnosis when a child's eating difficulties have clearly associated sensory reactivity or processing and/or motor difficulties. If the difficulties are accompanied by notable sensory-motor problems such as tactile hypersensitivity (e.g., rejection of certain food textures) and/or low oral-muscle tone (e.g. the child will only eat soft foods), then the specific regulatory subtypes should be considered. If organic/structural problems (e.g. cleft palate, reflux, etc.) affect the child's ability to eat or digest food, eating behavior disorder should not be used as a primary diagnosis and the appropriate medical diagnosis can be indicated under Axis III. However, if an eating disturbance which may have originated in organic or structural difficulties continues after these initial difficulties have been resolved, the diagnosis of eating behavior disorder may be appropriate.

This category should not be used as a primary diagnosis when a child's eating disturbances are part of a larger symptom picture, associated with other affective or behavioral disturbances related to primary relationships, trauma, or other adjustment difficulties. When the primary reason for the disruption of eating is related to other emotional issues, the child's eating disregulation will be classified according to the emotional dynamics and relationship issues which accompany it. To capture such patterns, the clinician should consider the affect disorders, particularly anxiety, reactive attachment disorder, etc.

This category should not be used as a primary diagnosis if irregular eating patterns or severely constricted food choices are part of multisystem developmental disorder and related patterns of rigidity and inability to take in new experiences.

700. Disorders of Relating and Communicating

This group of disorders is first evident in infancy and early childhood. These disorders involve severe difficulties in relating and communicating, combined with difficulties in the regulation of physiological, sensory, attentional, motor, cognitive, somatic, and affective processes.

Historically, children with the most severe types of difficulties in relating and communicating were described as evidencing Autistic Disorder. Kanner's original description (Kanner, L., Autistic disturbances of affective contact, *Nervous Child 2*, 1943: 217-250) focused on a basic impairment in relating as the definitive feature: "From the beginning, an extreme autistic aloneness that disregards, ignores, shuts out...anything from the outside." (p. 247). The various editions of the Diagnostic and Statistical Manual (DSM) of the American Psychiatric Association up through DSM-III-R and DSM IV affirm this view. "This impairment is characterized by failure to develop interpersonal relationships and by lack of responsiveness to, or interest in, people," including in infancy, "by a failure to cuddle, by lack of eye contact and facial responsiveness, and by indifference or aversion to affection and physical contact." (DSM III-R, p. 34).

Over time, children who had some, but not all, of the characteristics of autistic disorder were described as Autistic Spectrum, Pervasive Developmental Disorder Not Otherwise Specified (PDD-NOS), Asperger's Syndrome, Childhood Disintegrative Psychosis, and Atypical. An expanded framework emerged, with Autistic Disorder as one of a group of disorders sharing common characteristics. In DSM III-R and DSM IV, for example, PDD-NOS is one of the disorders in this group for children who do not meet all the criteria for Autistic Disorder. In DSM IV, the Pervasive Developmental Disorders expanded to include Autistic Disorder, Disintegrative Disorder, Asperger's Syndrome, Rett's Syndrome, and PDD-NOS.

The shift to a broader definition of the syndrome is understandable in light of clinical experience reflecting a range of relationship and communication problems in children who share some of the traditionally described Autistic features. The important question is: Should the children who evidence only relative impairments in relating and communicating, and demonstrate clear capacities for not insignificant degrees of emotional intimacy with familiar caregivers, as is the case with many children diagnosed PDD-NOS or Asperger's Syndrome, be considered part of the same group as children who historically have been described as completely lacking the capacity for interpersonal relating?

PDD-NOS is not well defined in DSM III-R or DSM IV. The definition only describes in the most general terms severe and pervasive impairments in relating, communicating, quality of interests, and the absence of sufficient criteria to meet the definition of the other categories in the group of disorders labeled PDD. Yet more and more children, particularly young children with a large range of language and interpersonal challenges, are being diagnosed as PDD-NOS. If these children, with a large array of developmental patterns and yet unknown potential developmental competencies, are considered as part of the same broad group as autism, is there the possibility for confusion regarding the course of this disorder and its prognosis? For example, will findings based on studies of traditional autism be applied to children with mixed features? Are there sufficient studies to clarify the differences in course and outcomes among types of PDD-NOS or between PDD-NOS and Autistic Disorder?

Because the prognosis associated with Autistic Disorder is quite pessimistic, the issue of which patterns should constitute a disorder and which disorders should be grouped together is of practical as well as conceptual importance. Many clinicians and parents, for example, form expectations for children with mixed features who are currently diagnosed as PDD-NOS based on data collected on children with Autistic Disorder. New studies looking at the prognosis of children with mixed features (e.g., PPD-NOS) are clearly needed in order to define this syndrome more clearly. Should children who evidence some capacity for relating along with communication, cognitive, motor, and sensory dysfunctions be initially considered in a separate group until there are more definitive studies on children with mixed features? Such studies may suggest a classification with more specific treatment and prognostic implications.

In considering these questions, clinicians and investigators should take emerging information into account. A growing body of clinical evidence suggests that children currently being diagnosed with Pervasive Developmental Disorder present a range of relationship patterns, differences in affect regulation, and a variety of processing and cognitive difficulties. Cognitive deficits have been suggested as playing a role in the etiology of Pervasive Developmental Disorders. Studies of biological differences, including prenatal and perinatal and anatomical, neurophysiologic, and neurochemical patterns, are for the most part non-specific and have not separated out relationship deficits, processing, and regulatory dysfunctions.

Furthermore, one sees children evidencing "autistic behaviors" in relationship to various combinations of uneven central nervous system maturation and functioning, and various environmental stresses. Children can move in and out of some of these worrisome behavioral patterns. In addition, some of the clinical features traditionally used to diagnose PDD-Autistic Spectrum Disorders are not unique to this syndrome. For example, motor patterns such as hand flapping, perseverative behavior, and echolalia can be seen in warmly related children with difficulties modulating motor tone and motor planning, sensory, auditory processing, and/or language dysfunctions.

Most importantly, when identified early and treated appropriately, many children with "autistic features" develop relationships of warmth and intimacy. Many children show a capacity to make consistent progress, especially in relating more warmly and interactively. Progress in language and cognitive development often follows improved relating.

The range of patterns and lack of specificity observed in children with marked difficulties in relating and communicating underscores the questions raised above. Should a large range of difficulties in relating and communicating be considered as part of one group of disorders which includes Autistic Disorder, or should children who evidence relative capacities for relating along with other communication, motor and sensory difficulties be considered as part of a separate group?

Rather than try to answer this question at this time, it is recommended that more experience be obtained to further understand children with a range of relationship and communication difficulties. In the interim, the clinician should consider two choices:

1. Use the DSM IV conceptualization Pervasive Developmental Disorder (PDD) or

2. Use Multisystem Developmental Disorder (MSDD), a conceptualization which does not consider the range of relationship and communication difficulties observed in clinical populations as part of the same broad group as children with Autistic Disorder. In MSDD the relationship difficulty is not viewed as a relatively fixed permanent deficit but as open to change and growth.

It is especially important to consider different alternatives for children in the first three years of life when development is rapid, naturally uneven, and potentially more flexible.

The category of Pervasive Developmental Disorders described in DSM IV includes Autistic Disorder as well as the additional subtypes of Rett's Disorder, Asperger's Disorder, Childhood Disintegrative Disorder, and Pervasive Developmental Disorder-Not Otherwise Specified. While PDD has a number of clinical features, the relationship deficit is viewed as primary, and is its defining characteristic. The relationship deficit is also viewed as relatively permanent, though with variations.

In contrast, the proposed category of Multisystem Developmental Disorder is based on the view that various degrees of difficulties in relating are seen in young children, but they are not on a continuum with a **primary** deficit in relating. This view leaves open the possibility that difficulties in relating, even when severe, may be **secondary** to motor and sensory processing deficits, such as difficulties in regulating, comprehending and responding to different types of sensations (including auditory and visual) and affects. For example, many infants and toddlers may avoid eye contact, ignore vocal and verbal overtures, and move away from caregivers. Yet as their sensory reactivity and processing difficulties improve, they seek out their caregivers more and more, initially to get things or help and later for closeness and intimacy. However, even when very avoidant, many of these infants and toddlers evidence subtle ways of showing their affective involvement with their caregivers (e.g., gets frightened if caregiver leaves room in a new setting, or favors caregiver for certain types of sensory experiences, such as deep pressure).

This view leaves open the possibility that when these patterns are identified early in the first two to three years of life (the earlier the better), the connection between the relationship capacity and the processing deficits may be more flexible. Therefore, in this view the possibility for progress and expectations regarding ultimate prognosis, including the possibility for warm relationships, logical thinking and problem solving, and interactive communication is not limited by the definition of the syndrome.

A definitive understanding of children with a range of severe relationship and communication problems will only emerge with further research. Meanwhile, it seems most prudent and useful to have a way to categorize these relationship and communication problems that leaves open the etiology, the course of development, and the prognosis. This approach seems especially important for children under age three, whose relationship capacities may be quite flexible.

Therefore, in addition to Pervasive Developmental Disorders, as described in DSM IV, this classification system, which focuses on infants and very young children offers the category termed Multisystem Developmental Disorder (MSDD). MSDD is simply a descriptive term, reflecting the fact that there are multiple types of delays or dysfunctions. The MSDD diagnosis should be considered for children who evidence a significant impairment in communication and motor and sensory processing but reveal some capacity or potential for intimacy and closeness in relating.

Before making the diagnosis of PDD **or** MSDD, a clinician should observe a child for a substantial period of time, together with the caregivers, in a supportive, safe, not overly stimulating setting, where spontaneous interaction and play are possible and encouraged. A skilled clinician should, with an appropriate warm-up period, also attempt to interact with the child for a reasonable period of time, using appropriate clinical skills to facilitate relating and communicating. The determination that a child cannot engage in relationships should only be made if the child is not observed relating to his caregivers **or** a skilled clinician over a substantial period of time, and preferably in multiple settings. A determination of relationship capacity should not be based predominantly on the clinician's interactions with a child, or on only incidental observations of the child's interactions with caregivers (e.g., during an interview with the parents, as sometimes is the case). In addition, the child's relationship to peers, while important, should not be used as a basis for determining his most basic capacity for relating. Observing a child's response to intervention over a period of time is the most useful way to gauge relationship potential.

Multisystem Developmental Disorder: The defining characteristics of Multisystem Developmental Disorder (MSDD) are:

1. Significant impairment in, but not complete lack of, the ability to engage in an emotional and social relationship with a primary caregiver, (e.g., may appear avoidant or aimless but may evidence subtle emergent forms of relating or relate quite warmly intermittently).

2. Significant impairment in forming, maintaining, and/or developing communication. This includes preverbal gestural communication, as well as verbal and nonverbal (e.g., figurative) symbolic communication.

3. Significant dysfunction in auditory processing (i.e., perception and comprehension).

4. Significant dysfunction in the processing of other sensations including hyper- and hypo-reactivity (e.g., to visual-spatial, tactile, proprioceptive, and vestibular input), and motor planning (e.g., sequencing movements).

The processing, relationship and communication difficulties described above are evidenced in various forms. Three patterns that are frequently observed are described, with the recognition that they are not yet intended to suggest specific subtypes, but to facilitate clinical identification, treatment planning and research. The three patterns below are characterized more specifically in Appendix 2. These patterns should not be diagnosed before the age at which one would normally expect the child to evidence the relative adaptive pattern in each.

701. Pattern A

These children are aimless and unrelated most of the time, with severe difficulty in motor planning, so that even simple intentional gestures are difficult. They usually show flat or inappropriate or unmodulated affect but at times, with direct sensory play, can evidence moments of pleasure or, if overstimulated, a tantrum. These children show a great deal of self-stimulation, rhythmic behaviors rather than more organized, perseverative behavior with objects. Many also have poor muscle tone and tend to be under-reactive to sensation, requiring more and more intense input to respond. These children may also have selective patterns of over-reactivity to sensation, such as touch or certain types of sound. Some children who evidence this pattern of aimless behavior do not have low motor tone but are overly active and extremely distractable.

With interventions that provide the necessary levels of sensory and affective involvement and deal with the under-reactivity and motor planning difficulties, these children may evidence gradually increasing relatedness and purposefulness.

702. Pattern B

These children are intermittently related and capable some of the time of simple intentional gestures. In this group the affect appears accessible, but fleeting, with small islands of shallow satisfaction or pleasure, but no consistent interpersonal joy or warmth. These children tend to enjoy repetitive or perseverative activity with objects (rather than only self-stimulation) but are very rigid and react intensely to any changes in their lives. Children who fit this pattern show mixed patterns of sensory reactivity and muscle tone, and are much more organized than children with pattern A in the way they seek sensation or avoid sensation. Most of the time they try to express their intentionality in patterns of negativism or purposeful avoidance. They often do this to control the amount of sensory and affective input they can take in.

With interventions that extend interactive sequences, these children may evidence increasingly complex behavioral and affective interactions.

703. Pattern C

These children evidence a more consistent sense of relatedness and can be very reactive to others even when they are avoidant or rigid. While they tend to avoid continuous relating, they have islands of warm pleasurable affect and relatedness, and are more consistently related than children in patterns A and B. They are able to use simple social gestures (e.g., reaching, looking, vocalizing, exchanging objects), and intermittently capable of complex interactive behavior and gestures (e.g., taking parent to the door to leave). These children also resist change, tending to be very perseverative and preoccupied with certain objects, but they will allow another individual to join them in their perseverative behavior and make it interactive (e.g., they will somewhat playfully try to remove your hand from the door, as they keep trying to open and close it repeatedly). They evidence a mixed pattern of sensory reactivity and motor planning difficulties, with a tendency towards over-reactivity to sensation. They may use some words or phrases in scripted or rote form, i.e., repeating words from a video or song.

With interventions that foster relating, encourage spontaneous affects and inclinations, prolong interactive sequences, and support symbolic elaboration of affects, these children may evidence continuous increases in intimacy, emotional expressiveness, and level of symbolic thinking.

Axis II: Relationship Disorder Classification

Understanding the quality of the parent-infant relationship is an important part of developing a diagnostic profile for infants and young children. The primary relationships of infants and young children contribute not only to the development of children's personality and structure of psychological defenses but also to young children's beliefs about what is possible to expect in relationships with others.

In infant mental health, the therapeutic work often focuses on the parent-infant relationship. Thus it is important to think about and conceptualize primary relationships as entities to be assessed, and when indicated, diagnosed. When a disorder exists, it is *specific to a relationship*. Clinicians can be assisted in systematically understanding the meaning of behaviors within the young child's primary relationship(s). Interventions can then be formulated and focused on both individual and relationship levels.

The relationship disorders described below have been set forth to characterize the nature of the disturbances seen in the specific relationships and interactions of infants and young children and their parents when things go awry. (Parent rather than caregiver is used in this axis to denote the intensity of the parent-child relationship, but in many cases another caregiver who is in the role of the parent, e.g., a grandparent or foster parent, should be considered in place of the biological parent.)

Parent-child relationship disorders are characterized by perceptions, attitudes, behaviors and affects of either the parent, the child or both, that result in disturbed parent-child interactions. The parent may relate with the infant from the beginning in light of his or her own personality dynamics, including projections and defenses. These may interact with distinct infant patterns and lead to relationship difficulties or disorders.

Diagnoses of relationship disturbances or disorders should be based not only on observed behavior but also on the parent's subjective experience of the child as expressed during a clinical interview. Where there are difficulties in the relationship, the **intensity**, **frequency** and **duration** of the disturbance are the factors that guide the clinician to classify the relationship problem as a perturbation, a disturbance, or a disorder.

Axis II should be used only to diagnose **significant** relationship difficulties. Clinicians should realize that an infant with a primary diagnosis (Axis I) need not have a relationship diagnosis (Axis II). The relationship axis does not address the full range of relationships, from well-adapted to disordered. Some parents may have tendencies in the directions described in Axis II — toward, for example, overinvolvement or hostility. Milder forms of relationship disorders may be triggered by the child's disorder, family dynamics or other stresses that challenge parents' usual balance between nurturance and more problematic parental functioning. However, clinicians should be careful not to overdiagnose a relationship disorder when such milder and transient forms related to stress are observed. The diagnostician may want to keep the described categories in mind when they appear in milder or transient forms in order to understand the dynamics of the family and to guide intervention.

The Parent Infant Relationship Global Assessment Scale (PIR-GAS), a research-based rating instrument found in the appendix, covers the full range of parent/infant relationships and can be used for research purposes to describe the strengths of a relationship as well as to capture the severity of a disorder. These ratings range from well-adapted (90) to grossly impaired (10). A rating **below 40** includes disordered, severely disordered and grossly impaired relationships. These qualify for a relationship diagnosis based on the severity and pervasiveness of the dyad's difficulties. At these levels the majority of the behaviors must be in evidence in an intense, ongoing and persistent manner. For ratings between **70-40**, the relationship tendencies or features may be usefully described, but are not severe enough to be considered a disorder.

There are three aspects of a relationship that are used in deciding whether there is a relationship disorder or not. These include:

• behavioral quality of the interaction;

• affective tone; and

• psychological involvement.

The behavioral qualities are required criteria for making the diagnosis since these are observable and of sufficient concern to assess and treat. The affective tone and psychological involvement are presented to elaborate and guide the user to the possible dynamics related to the behaviors worthy of further exploration and treatment.

Behavioral quality of the interaction is reflected in the behavior of each member of the parent-infant dyad. The behavior of the parent, the child, or both may be disturbed. Sensitivity or insensitivity in responding to infant's cues, contingent or non-contingent responsivity, genuineness of involvement or concern, regulation, predictability, and the quality of structuring and mediating of the environment are parental behaviors that contribute to the quality of the interaction. Averting, avoiding, arching, lethargy, nonresponsiveness, and defiance are examples of behaviors which infants may bring to the interaction. At times it is not clear whether the behaviors of concern are initiated or reactive. For instance, a mother or father may look depressed, uninvolved or unresponsive with the infant. However, this may in part be a result of the unfocused gaze and other unresponsive, non-reinforcing behavior of a medically ill infant.

Disturbances in infants and young children may also appear as delays in development (language, motor, cognition, or social-emotional), and may constrict the child's interactive capacities. These delays may be both the result of and contribute to the relationship disturbance.

Affective tone refers to the emotional tone characteristic of this dyad. Intense anxious/tense or negative affect (i.e.,irritable, angry, hostile) on the part of either member of the dyad or both may contribute to the characteristic affect tone of the dyad. The concern here is the dysregulating function of intense affect and the uncertainty as to what may happen next that is conveyed when intense affect is present.

Psychological involvement is focused on parental attitudes and perceptions of the child (i.e. the meaning of the child's behavior to the parents). The parents' image of a caregiving relationship developed from past experiences in early childhood relationships usually influences the parents' perceptions of a particular child and what can be expected in a relationship. Disturbing or adverse past experiences may result in a parent misinterpreting and inferring these feelings as part of his or her infant (e.g., the parent may misinterpret certain behaviors of the infant as demanding, negative or attacking).

Only one relationship diagnosis should be chosen whenever possible. Occasionally there may be a relationship where no one feature predominates and several of the features described below apply. In such cases, a mixed category can be identified, specifying the specific features of the relationship. For example, the relationship may appear overinvolved and overprotective, but is actually emotionally distant and aloof. If any form of abuse is involved, i.e., verbal, physical or sexual as described in detail below, the diagnosis of an abusive relationship takes precedence over any other relationship diagnosis. However, the other features most characteristic of the relationship should be described.

901. Overinvolved:

Relationship may be characterized by physical and/or psychological overinvolvement

A. Behavioral Quality of Interaction

1. Parent often interferes with infant's goals and desires.

2. Parent dominates infant through over-control.

3. Parent makes developmentally inappropriate demands.

4. Infant may appear diffuse, unfocused and undifferentiated.

5. Infant may display submissive, overly compliant behaviors or, conversely, defiant behaviors.

6. Infant may evidence a lack of motor skills and/or language expressiveness.

B. Affective Tone

1. The parent may have periods of anxiety, depression, or anger which result in a lack of consistency in the parent-infant interaction.

2. Infant may passively or actively express anger/obstinacy and whine.

C. Psychological Involvement

1. The parent may perceive the infant as a partner or peer or may romanticize or eroticize the infant.

2. The parent does not see infant as a separate individual with his or her own needs and lacks genuine interest in the infant's uniqueness. This may include diffuse generational boundaries. Examples include:

   a. Attempts by the parent to involve the infant in meeting the parent's own needs.

   b. Using the infant or young child as a confidante.

   c. Extreme physical closeness or eroticized touch.

   d. A low level of reciprocity or dialogue, suggesting no clear sense of two separate individuals.

902. Underinvolved:

Relationship may be characterized by sporadic or infrequent genuine involvement or connectedness with infant, often reflected in a lack of concern or low quality of care.

A. Behavioral Quality of Interaction

1. The parent is insensitive and/or unresponsive to infant's cues.

   For example, a depressed parent may express love and concern for his or her infant verbally but be too tired or withdrawn to be emotionally available for the crying infant.

2. There is an observed lack of consistency between the parent's expressed attitudes about the infant and the quality of actual interactions. Evidence of predictability or reciprocity in the order and sequence of interactions may be missing.

   For example, a parent may verbally express concern about the need for food of an infant who is failing to thrive, while restricting the infant's feedings.

3. The parent ignores, rejects, or fails to comfort the infant.

4. The parent does not adequately mirror infant's behavior through appropriate reflection of the infant's internal feeling states.

5. The parent does not adequately protect the infant from sources of physical or emotional harm or abuse by others.

   For example:

   a. The parent leaves the infant alone for extended periods of time or in the care of a young sibling.

   b. The home environment is not infant-proofed.

6. Parent-infant interactions are observed to be under-regulated, as the infant's cues are often missed or misinterpreted by the parent.

7. The parent and infant often appear to be disengaged and/or have only intermittent connections.

   For example, little eye contact or physical proximity is noted.

8. The infant may appear physically and/or psychologically uncared for.

   For example:

   a. The child is frequently ill, and there is a history of a lack of regular medical care.

   b. The child's body or clothing is dirty.

   c. Nonorganic failure to thrive.

9. The infant may appear delayed in motor and language skills due to lack of nurturing support for development. However, some children may be precocious in motor and language skills, using these capacities as part of a promiscuous character style with adults.

B.   Affective Tone

1.   Affect in both parent and infant is often constricted, withdrawn, sad, and flat.

2.   To the observer, the interaction suggests lifelessness and an absence of pleasure.

C.   Psychological Involvement

1.   The parent may not demonstrate awareness of infant's cues or needs in discussions with others, or in interactions with the infant.

2.   A parent's own relationship history may have been characterized by emotional deprivation and/or physical neglect. As a consequence the parent may be unaware of an infant's needs.

For example, a parent is often/regularly physically and/or emotionally unavailable and has not provided for consistent substitute care for the infant or toddler.

903.   Anxious/Tense:

This relationship is characterized by interactions which are tense, constricted, with little sense of relaxed enjoyment or mutuality. The relationship provides an affective communication to the clinician of anxiety/tension.

A.   Behavioral Quality of Interaction

1.   Parent's sensitivity to cues is often extremely heightened.

2.   The parent expresses frequent concerns regarding infant's well-being, behavior or development and may be overprotective.

3.   Physical handling of infant may be awkward or tense.

4.   The relationship may involve verbally/emotionally negative interactions, but these are not the primary quality of the relationship.

5.   There is a poor fit between infant's and parent's temperament or activity level.

6.   The infant may be very compliant or anxious around the parent.

For example, an infant or toddler is excessively clingy to parent, or the infant's anxiety interferes with expected developmental abilities, such as articulating speech or pretend play.

B.   Affective Tone

1.   The parent or infant exhibits an anxious mood—as seen in motor tension, apprehension, agitation, facial expressions, and quality of vocalization or speech.

1. Both parent and infant overreact. Therefore they overreact to each other. This leads to an escalation of disregulating interactions. This pattern is often seen coexisting with underlying regulatory difficulties in the child.

C. Psychological Involvement

The parent often misinterprets the child's behavior and/or affect and a consequently responds inappropriately to the child.

For example, a parent whose toddler cries and screams may perceive the infant's distress or frustration as a response to his or her incompetence as a parent. The parent may experience feelings of rejection and feelings of failure, and then may blame and withdraw from the infant.

904. Angry/Hostile:

This relationship is characterized by parent-infant interactions which are harsh and abrupt, often lacking in emotional reciprocity. The relationship conveys to the clinician an affective communication of anger/hostility.

A. Behavioral Quality of the Interaction

1. The parent may be insensitive to the infant's cues, especially when the infant is viewed as demanding.
2. Physical handling of the infant is abrupt.
3. The parent may taunt or tease the infant.
4. The infant may appear frightened, anxious, inhibited, impulsive, or diffusely aggressive.
5. The young child may exhibit defiant or resistant behavior with the parent.
6. The child may exhibit demanding and/or aggressive behaviors with the parent.
7. The child may exhibit fearful, vigilant and avoidant behaviors.
8. The child may show a tendency toward concrete behavior rather than the development of fantasy and imagination. Certain aspects of cognition and language having to do with forming abstractions, as well as coping with complex feelings, may be inhibited or delayed.

B. Affective Tone

1. Interaction between parent and child typically has a hostile or angry edge.
2. Moderate to considerable tension between parent and infant is observed, with a noticeable lack of enjoyment or enthusiasm.
3. The child's affect may be constricted.

C. Psychological Involvement

The parent may view the child's dependence as demanding and resent the child's needs. This resentment may be due to current life stressors or stem from the parent's own relationship history, which may have been characterized by emotional deprivation and/or hostility. Examples include:

a. The parent may see the infant's dependency needs as similar to the neediness of the parent's own depressed, unavailable or angry parent in the past. As a result the parent may respond with frustration or anger to the infant's needs.

b. The parent may view the child's increasing independence, assertiveness or age appropriate negativity as threatening to his or her authority or control.

c. The parent may project his or her own negative feelings onto the infant and then interact with the infant as if the infant embodied these feelings.

905. Mixed Relationship Disorder:

The relationship may be characterized by a combination of the features described above.

In some parent-infant relationships, no one pattern of problematic interaction seems to predominate. The category of mixed relationship disorder can be used to classify such relationships. When using this category, the clinician should identify the specific patterns observed — for example, alternation between angry, hostile interactions and distant, underinvolved interactions, or vacillation between over- and under-protectiveness.

906. Abusive:

Abuse may be verbal, physical, and/or sexual. The following three diagnoses relate to specific forms of abuse and take precedence over the relationship diagnoses above. If any of these apply, the clinician should use them as the primary relationship diagnosis and then characterize the ongoing overall pattern of the relationship using one of the above relationship descriptions (e.g. underinvolved, angry/tense, etc.)

Because of the level of severity and persistence of abusive behaviors, **one** descriptor from Behavioral Quality of Interaction is sufficient to make this diagnosis for any form of abuse. Of course, more than one may apply.

906a. Verbally Abusive:

Involves severe abusive emotional content, unclear boundaries, and overcontrol.

A. Behavioral Quality of the Interaction

1. The content of verbal/emotional abuse by the parent is intended to severely belittle, blame, attack, overcontrol and reject the infant or toddler.

2. The infant or toddler's reactions may vary widely, from constriction and vigilance to severe acting-out behaviors (This variation will depend on the parent's projective contents and the infant's temperament and developmental level).

B. Affective Tone

1. The negative, abusive nature of the parent-infant interaction may be reflected in the infant's depressed, disregulated and/or sober affect.

C. Psychological Involvement

1. The parent may misinterpret the infant's cries, often viewing these as deliberate negative reactions towards himself or herself. This misinterpretation may be observed in the verbal content of the parent's attacks, which reflect unresolved issues in previous critical relationships.

2. Input from the infant may stir up early painful experiences, such as in the case of a mother who cannot bring herself to respond to her infant's cries due to her own experiences of neglect, or who feels inadequate and unworthy when unable to comfort the infant. This connection is often not conscious.

906b. Physically Abusive:

A. Behavioral Quality of Interaction

1. The parent physically harms the infant or child.
   Examples include:
   a. Slapping, spanking, hitting, pinching, biting, and kicking.
   b. Physical restraint.
   c. Isolation for extensive periods.
   d. Other extreme forms of punishment.

2. The parent regularly denies the infant or child essentials for survival, including food, medical care, and/or opportunity to rest.

3. This diagnosis may also include periods of verbal/emotional abuse and/or sexual abuse.

B. Affective Tone

1. Anger, hostility, or irritability in emotional tone of dyad.

2. Considerable to moderate tension and anxiety between parent and infant, with a noticeable lack of enjoyment or enthusiasm.

C. Psychological Involvement

1. The parent exhibits and/or describes anger or hostility towards the infant through abrupt voice or behavior (e.g., scowls, frowns, exhibits harsh punitive verbal content and/or attitude.) The parent exhibits difficulty setting limits in a non-attacking manner.

2. The child may evidence a tendency toward concrete behavior rather than the development of fantasy and imagination. Certain aspects of cognition and language having to do with forming abstractions, as well as coping with complex feelings, may be inhibited or delayed.

3. The interaction may include periods of closeness or enmeshment and of distance, avoidance or hostility.

4. Parent and infant may function reasonably well in certain areas, but become either too involved or too distant around certain "triggering" issues (e.g., past experiences or internal representations of relationships in the parent's history make the parent project, or misinterpret certain behaviors of infant as demanding, negative or attacking.

906c. Sexually Abusive:

Involves a lack of regard for physical boundaries and extreme sexualized intrusiveness.

A. Behavioral Quality

1. The parent engages in sexually seductive and overstimulating behavior with the infant or young child. The behaviors are intended to gratify the adult's sexual needs or desires.

    Examples include:

    a. Coercing or forcing the infant or toddler to touch parent sexually.

    b. Coercing or forcing the infant or toddler to accept sexual touching from parent.

    c. Coercing or forcing the infant or toddler to observe sexual behaviors of others.

2. The young child may evidence sexually driven behaviors such as exhibiting himself or trying to look at or touch other children.

3. This diagnosis may also include periods of verbal/emotional abuse and/or physical abuse.

B. Affective Tone

1. The lack of boundaries and consistency in parent-infant interaction may be reflected in the parent's affect, which may be labile. Periods of anger or anxiety may be observable.

2. The infant may appear anxious and/or tense.

3. The young child may be fearful, anxious, or diffusely aggressive.

C. Psychological Involvement

1. The parent characteristically does not respond empathically to the infant's needs and cues, due to preoccupation with his or her own needs for narcissistic self-gratification.

2. The parent has and may evidence extremely distorted thinking, permitting choice of the young infant as a sexual object.

It is also noteworthy the young child may evidence difficulties in developmental capacities for fantasy and imagination, as well as in developing the capacities for forming abstract categories in language and cognitive functioning. He or she may develop a tendency to form non-integrated organization of affect, thought and behavior, e.g., ego splitting rather than cohesive personality organization.

Axis III: Medical and Developmental Disorders and Conditions

Axis III should be used to note any physical (including medical and neurological), mental health, and/or developmental diagnoses made using other diagnostic and classification systems. These systems include the American Psychiatric Association's *Diagnostic and Statistical Manual* (DSM IV), *International Classification of Diseases* (ICD-9 or ICD-10), and specific classifications used by speech/language pathologists, occupational therapists, physical therapists, and special educators. A diagnostic and statistical manual for primary care providers (child version) is under development; the American Academy of Pediatrics' Task Force on Coding for Mental Health in Children is coordinating this effort.

Axis IV: Psychosocial Stressors

This axis is included to help clinicians take into account various forms and severity of psychosocial stress that are **influencing** factors in a variety of disorders in infancy and early childhood. (In contrast, in traumatic stress disorders described in Axis I, acute or chronic stress is the **critical** factor responsible for the disorder.)

Psychosocial stress may be present in the life of an infant or young child either directly (for example, an illness in the child requiring hospitalization) or indirectly (for example, a sudden illness in the parent that results in separation). Psychosocial stress may be acute or enduring; it may have a single source or involve multiple and cumulative events. Specific events and transitions that are part of normal experience in the culture may be stressful for an infant or young child — for example, the birth of a sibling, a family move, a parent returning to work after being at home, or entry into child care or preschool. Some children will experience these transitions as stressful while others make transitions smoothly and adapt to new circumstances easily. Other sources of stress are pervasive and enduring; these include poverty, violence in the environment, and abuse in the home.

In considering the impact of direct and indirect psychosocial stress on infants and young children, it is useful to think in terms of the child's loss of basic safety, security, and comfort — that is, the protective, supportive "envelope" that should constitute an infant's immediate caregiving environment. Thus the clinician must distinguish the severity of a specific type of stressor from its ultimate impact on the child, which will be modified by the response of the environment. The caregiving environment may shield and protect the child from the stressor, thus lessening its impact; it may compound the impact by failing to offer protection; or it may reinforce the impact of the stressor through the effect of anxiety and/or other negative attitudes.

The ultimate impact of a stressful event or enduring stress depends on three factors:

- the severity of the stressor (its intensity and duration at that level of intensity; the suddenness of the initial stress; and the frequency and unpredictability of its recurrence);
- the developmental level of the child (chronological age, endowment, and ego strength); and
- the availability and capacity of adults in the caregiving environment to serve as a protective buffer and help the child understand and deal with the stressor.

The purpose of the stress index below is to identify sources of stress, their severity, and their duration with respect to an individual infant or young child. The greater the number of factors involved, the greater the stress on the child is presumed to be. The effects of stress which should be considered include disruptions in development, symptomatic behaviors, regressions, psychic trauma behaviors, changes in affect, and relationship difficulties. The purpose of assessing the overall impact of stress on an infant includes an attempt to capture the child's resilience in light of the amount of stress, individual capacities (inner resources), and outside support. The other axes in this classification system will capture the specific nature of the impact on the infant.

In view of the rapidly changing progression of developmental steps and biological maturation in the earliest years, and the infant's relative sensitivity to change and ability to adapt or maladapt, we propose the following definitions for "predominantly acute" and "predominantly enduring" stress:

Predominantly Acute	*Predominantly Enduring*
Year One: under one month	beyond one month
Year Two: under three months	beyond three months
Year Three: under three months	beyond three months

To use the index, the clinician should identify all the sources of stress and determine the severity of the stress (rated from mild to severe). Then rate the impact of the stress on the child, which may be modified by the reaction of the environment, which may shield or compound the impact.

In order to capture the cumulative severity of the stress, it is important to identify **all** the sources of stress in a child's circumstances — for example, a child in foster placement may also be experiencing the impact of abuse, parental psychiatric illness, separation, and poverty. Similarly, the clinician should be sure to identify current normal sources of stress, whether or not they are having a negative effect — for example, a family move, birth of a sibling, entry into school/child care, etc.

Stress Index

Sources of Stress	*Acute*	*Enduring*
Abduction		
Abuse - physical		
Abuse - sexual		
Abuse - emotional		
Adoption		
Birth of sibling		
Foster placement		
Hospitalization		
Loss of parent		
Loss of significant other		
Medical illness		
Move		
Natural disaster		
Neglect		
Parent illness - medical		
Parent illness - psychiatric		
Poverty		
School/child care entry		
Separation from parent-work		
Separation from parent-other		
Sudden loss of home		
Sudden injury		
Trauma to significant other		
Violence in environment		
Other		
Number of stressors		

Overall Impact of Stress:

The clinician should consider the overall impact on the infant of all the stressors listed above given the protective response of the milieu. The list below can be used as a rating scale for clinical or research purposes.

1. No obvious effects

2. Mild effects — causes recognizable strain, tension or anxiety but does not interfere with infant's overall adaptation, e.g., irritability, temporary bursts of anger or crying, shifts in sleep, etc.

5. Moderate effects — derails child in areas of adaptation but not in core areas of relatedness and communication, e.g., clings to mother, does not want to go to school or child care, oppositional or impulsive behavior, sleep disturbances, etc.

7. Severe effects — significant derailment in areas of adaptation, e.g., infant pulls away from relationships, appears depressed and withdrawn, inconsolable crying, terrified, cannot communicate, etc.

Axis V: Functional Emotional Developmental Level

The fifth axis of this multiaxial diagnostic approach addresses the way in which the infant organizes experience, reflected in his or her functioning. Can the young child, for example, organize experience into a mental representation (a multisensory symbolic picture) as seen in pretend play, or is the infant at the mercy of behavioral discharge? The developmental level at which the infant organizes affective, interactive, communicative, cognitive, motor and sensory experience is designated on this Axis.

In this scheme, developmental level constitutes a number of basic interrelated processes which emerge developmentally following each other, but each of which continues to develop and become more complex as the child grows older. For example, mutual attention develops first and both lengthens in duration and is sustained under more complex conditions and behavior as the infant develops. The three month old may look and follow her parent for 5 -10 seconds, can do so while also showing pleasure and engagement for 30 seconds a few months later, and will continue at 10 or 11 months to attend, enjoy, and may also transfer an object back and forth while "playing" for a minute or two.

As the infant becomes capable of each of the processes, it is important to evaluate whether the child has reached the age-expected functional developmental level. It is also useful to assess the conditions under which the child can show mastery of this level. For example, an infant may be able to attend, engage, and interact reciprocally with a parent when the environment is quiet. In contrast, in a noisy environment, this infant may tune out, wander off, or choose to play with a toy, disregarding the people around him.

The essential processes or capacities constituting each functional developmental level follow. The age range at which each ability begins to develop is also indicated.

Mutual Attention: All ages

Capacity to show interest in the world by looking and listening when talked to or provided with appropriate visual, auditory, movement and tactile experiences. The ability of the dyad to attend to one another and remain calm and focused for a reasonable period of time depends on the age of the infant, e.g., 5+ seconds by 3-4 months, 30+ seconds by 8-10 months, 2+ minutes by two years of age, and 15 minutes by four years.

Mutual Engagement: Readily observable between 3-6 months.

Ability for joint emotional involvement, seen in looking, joyful smiling and laughing, synchronous arm and leg movements, and other gestures which convey a sense of pleasure and affective engagement. This is usually well established by 4-6 months. As the relationship evolves, the infant evidences a growing sense of security and comfort, and interest and curiosity in the caregiver. As development proceeds, a fuller range of emotions becomes part of this capacity.

Interactive Intentionality and Reciprocity: Readily observable between six and eight months.

Ability to interact in a purposeful, intentional and reciprocal manner, both initiating and responding to the other's signals. The capacity for cause-and - effect interacting involves both sensorimotor patterns and different emotional inclinations, e.g. reaching out to be picked up, curiosity and exploring, pleasure in putting a finger in mommy's mouth, expressing anger and protest, etc. This may be thought of as opening and closing circles of communication. The infant initiates with, for example, looking at an object (opens the circle of communication), the parent responds with picking up the object and putting it right in front of the infant with a big smile and, "Here it is!" When the infant either vocalizes or reaches or changes her facial expression, she is closing the circle of communication by building on the parent's response. This capacity is usually established by 8 months. The number and complexity of interactions will increase as the child grows, from closing 3-4 circles by 8-10 months, to 10-15 circles by 12-16 months, to 20-30 circles by 20-24 months. This capacity should increase as the child grows from 2-3 years (30-40 circles) to 3-4 years (50+ circles).

Representational/Affective Communication: Infants over 18 months.

Capacity to use mental representations, as evidenced in language or pretend play, for communicating emotional themes and ideas. For example, the child pretending to feed or put baby to bed, crash cars, etc. at 18 to 24 months, with more elaboration and simple language, e.g. "me mad," "love you," by 30 months. At first gestures and language may be concrete and functional, related to daily experiences and routines.

Representational Elaboration: Children over 30 months.

Capacity to elaborate, in both make-believe and symbolic communication, a number of ideas that go beyond the basic needs and simple themes typical of early representational communication above. The child will evidence the capacity to use symbolic communication to convey two or more emotional ideas at a time in terms of more complex intentions, wishes, or feelings, e.g., themes of closeness or dependency, separation, exploration, assertiveness, anger, self pride or showing off. The ideas need not be related or logically connected to one another, e.g., trucks are crashing and then load up blocks to build a house.

Representational Differentiation I: Children over 36 months.

Capacity to deal with complex intentions, wishes and feelings in pretend play or other types of symbolic communication which involves two or more ideas which are logically connected. The child can distinguish the real from the unreal and is able to switch back and forth between fantasy and reality with little difficulty. By 36 months the child can close symbolic circles of communication in pretend play as well as in reality conversations.

Representational Differentiation II: Children over 42 months.

Capacity for elaborating complex pretend play and symbolic communication dealing with complex intentions, wishes, or feelings. The play or direct communication involves three or more ideas that are logically connected, the child can distinguish between reality and fantasy, and take into account concepts of causality, time and space. By 42-48 months, the child can plan "how," "what," and "why" elaborations that give depth to the drama or reality-based dialogues.

Guidelines for assessing functional emotional developmental level

The assessment of this axis should be based on observations of the infant interacting with each of her or his parents or other significant caretakers. Toward the end of the evaluation the diagnostician should also evaluate the quality of his or her own interaction with the infant and indicate levels reached.

Infants and young children vary in the length of time they can sustain these processes, as well as to the conditions needed for optimal engagement, i.e. to maintain the quality of the relating. For example, infants who are highly reactive or sensitive to various sensations and distractions may not be able to sustain mutual attention or reciprocity unless the parent changes to a quieter environment and woos them back into interaction. Or infants who are under-responsive to input or may overfocus on playing with toys rather than with their parents may not become affectively engaged (as would be evidenced by mutual gaze and pleasure) unless the parent provides sensorimotor contact to establish some mutuality.

It is important to note that while these processes initially emerge in a developmental progression, once past the expected age, an infant, toddler or young child may show these processes to different degrees.

Specifically, to evaluate functional emotional developmental level, the clinician needs to consider the following questions for each level:

- Has the infant reached his or her expected age capacities with regard to the functions?

- Can the infant respond at age-appropriate levels under a variety of conditions, including various affect states, such as pleasure, anger, frustration, etc., or under stress, or when the environment is confused, overstimulating, etc.?

- Can the infant respond more appropriately when the parent supports the interaction by providing sensory-motor facilitation (for example, swinging, bouncing, joint compression, singing)?

- Can the infant respond more appropriately when the parent controls the level of stress or confusion in the environment by reducing the level of stimulation (noise, lights, number of people or toys, etc.)?

- Does the parent need to be especially gifted, or can the child initiate age appropriate interactions (e.g.,rich pretend sequences)?

- Can child hold his own in an elaborate reality-based conversation?

In other words, the clinician should evaluate the developmental functional levels the child has reached, whether they are age-appropriate, how long they can be sustained, and the conditions needed for the child to be fully engaged in them.

Functional Emotional Developmental Level

There are two steps to determining the functional developmental level. The first requires evaluating the quality of the child's play and interaction with each of the significant people in her or his life. Identify all the specific levels the child has reached and with whom. The second step requires summarizing the overall functional level. Both are described below.

Evaluating the quality of the child's play and interaction

Consider the following levels in observing the child interact with each parent, other caregiver, and evaluator. These can also be treated as ratings for clinical and research purposes. Each person should be asked to interact or play with the child as they usually do for about ten minutes without interruption. For children two and older, if necessary, encourage the parent to play with toys or try "pretend" play after five minutes. Be sure to have appropriate toys available. Note: As the child gets older you will need to evaluate the current as well as earlier levels.

1. Age-appropriate level under all conditions and with full range of affect states.

2. Age-appropriate level but vulnerable to stress and/or with constricted range of affects

3. Has the capacity but not in keeping with age-expected forms of the capacity, e.g., relates but immaturely.

4. Needs some structure or sensorimotor support to evidence capacity; otherwise manifests capacity intermittently/inconsistently.

5. Barely evidences this capacity even with support.

6. Has not reached this level.

NA Not applicable (i.e., child is below the age she/he is expected to have this capacity).

Functional Emotional Developmental Level:

	Mother	Father	Other	Evaluator

Mutual attention: Ability of dyad to attend to one another (all ages)

Mutual engagement Ability for joint emotional involvement, seen in looks, gestures, etc. (3-6 months)

Interactive intentionality and reciprocity: Ability for cause and effect interaction where infant signals and responds purposefully to another person's signals; involves sensorimotor patterns and a range of emotional inclinations (6-18months)

Representational/affective communication: Capacity to use mental representations, as evidenced in language and play, to communicate emotional themes (over 18 months)

Representational elaboration: Ability to elaborate a number of ideas in pretend play and symbolic communication, that go beyond basic needs and deal with more complex intentions, wishes or feelings; ideas need not be logically connected (over 30 months)

Representational differentiation I: Ability to deal with complex intentions, wishes and feelings in pretend play and symbolic communication in which ideas are logically related; knows what is real and unreal and switches between fantasy and reality (over 36 months)

Representational differentiation II: Ability to elaborate complex pretend play and symbolic communication, characterized by three or more ideas logically connected and informed by concepts of causality, time and space (over 42 months)

Functional Emotional Developmental Level Summary

A summary assessment of functional emotional developmental level is based primarily on direct observation of and interaction with the child, but it is also important to ask about the child's functioning at home and at other times before determining the overall level. It is based on the child's most optimal functioning even if this level is not consistent with all caregivers. The child's inconsistency should be taken into account when determining the overall level.

1. Has fully reached expected levels.

2. At expected level but with constrictions:

   a. Does not function at this level in the full range of affect, e.g., closeness, assertion, anger, fear and anxiety.

   b. Does not function at this level under stress.

   c. Functions at this level only with certain caregivers and not with others, even though they are reasonably skillful, or with exceptional support.

3. Has not achieved current expected level but has achieved all prior levels (indicate which).

4. Has not achieved current expected level but has achieved some prior levels (indicate which).

5. Has not mastered any prior levels.

Appendix 1

Parent-Infant Relationship Global Assessment Scale (PIR-GAS)

This scale is to be used to assess the quality of the infant-parent relationship and ranges from well adapted to severely impaired. In general, it is expected that the scale will be completed after a clinical evaluation of an infant problem. Relationship problems may co-occur with symptomatic behaviors in the infant but are not synonymous with them. This means that serious symptoms may be apparent in an infant without relationship pathology, and relationships may be pathological without overt symptoms in the infant. The reason for relationship problems need not be known to use the scale, but they may derive from within the infant, from within the caregiver, from the unique "fit" between infant and caregiver, or from the larger social context. Stressors impinging on the relationship may be etiologically significant, but what is coded is only the pattern of the relationship, not the magnitude of the stressor.

90 Well Adapted:

Relationships in this range are functioning exceptionally well. They are not only mutually enjoyable and unusually conflict free, but they are also growth promoting for both partners' development.

80 Adapted:

Relationships in this range of functioning evidence no significant psychopathology. They are characterized by interactions that are frequently reciprocal and synchronous and are reasonably enjoyable. The developmental progress of the partners is not impeded in any way by the pattern of the relationship, which is "good enough" for both partners.

70 Perturbed:

Relationships in this range are functioning less than optimally in some way. The disturbance is limited to one domain of functioning and overall the relationship still functions reasonably well. The disturbance lasts from a few days to a few weeks.

For example: an infant with a minor physical illness sleeps poorly for several nights, exhausting his parents; or parents moving into a new house are less attentive to their infant, who is less able to self-regulate in the unfamiliar new surroundings.

60 Significantly Perturbed:

Relationships in this range of functioning are strained in some way but are still largely adequate and satisfying to the partners. The disturbance is not pervasive across a large number of domains, but instead, limited to one or two problematic areas. Further, the dyad seems likely to negotiate the challenge successfully and the pattern not to be enduring. The disturbance lasts no longer than a month. Caregivers may be stressed by the perturbation, but they are generally not overconcerned about the changed relationship pattern, instead considering it within the range of expectable responses that are likely to be relatively short-lived.

For example: a toddler develops food refusal for the first time following the birth of a new sibling.

50 Distressed:

Relationships in this range of functioning are more than transiently affected, but they still maintain some flexibility and adaptive qualities. One or both partners may be experiencing some distress in the context of the relationship, and the developmental progress of the dyad seems likely to be impeded if the pattern does not improve. Caregivers may or may not be concerned about the disturbed relationship pattern, but overt symptoms resulting from the disturbance in either partner are unlikely.

For example: A child is distressed frequently when her mother ignores her cues to slow down during feedings and face-to-face interactions. Other domains of functioning show no interaction problems nor child distress.

40 Disturbed:

Relationships in this range of functioning appear to place the dyad at significant risk for dysfunction. The relationship's adaptive qualities are beginning to be overshadowed by problematic features of the relationship. Although not deeply entrenched, the patterns appear more than transient and are beginning to adversely affect the subjective experience of one or both partners.

For example: Parent and child engage in excessive teasing and power struggles in multiple domains including, feeding, dressing, and bedtime. Although parent and child attempt pleasurable interactions, they often go too far, leaving one or both partners distressed.

30 Disordered:

Relationships in this range of functioning are characterized by relatively stable, maladaptive interactions and distress in one or both partners within the context of the relationship. Rigidly maladaptive interactions, particularly if they involve distress in one or both partners, are the hallmark of disordered relationships. Although generally conflicted, interactions in disordered relationships may instead be grossly inappropriate developmentally without overt conflicts.

For example: A depressed parent repeatedly seeks comfort from his or her infant, actively recruiting caregiving behavior from the child.

20 Severely Disordered:

Relationships in this range of functioning are severely compromised. One or more likely both partners are significantly distressed by the relationship itself. Maladaptive interactive patterns are rigidly entrenched, appear to be relatively impervious to change, and seem to be of relatively long duration, although the onset may be insidious. A significant proportion of interactions is almost always conflicted.

For example: A father and his toddler frequently interact in a conflicted manner. The father sets no limits until he becomes enraged and then he spanks the toddler vigorously. The toddler is provocative, and the father feels angry with him all the time.

10 Grossly Impaired:

Relationships in this range of functioning are dangerously disorganized. Interactions are disturbed so frequently that the infant is in imminent danger of physical harm.

Appendix 2

Multisystem Developmental Disorder

The following is a suggested set of descriptive criteria for three patterns of multisystem developmental disorder.

Because children are not expected to evidence certain social behaviors (e.g., simple and complex gestures) until certain ages, the following guidelines should be considered. A classification of Pattern A can be made only on an infant over five months of age (when simple gestures and intentional communication can begin to be expected). A classification of Pattern B can be made in an infant over nine months of age. A classification of Pattern C can be made in a child over 15 months of age.

Pattern A:

Relatedness and Interaction: These children appear most unrelated and aimless. They can only be engaged via direct sensory involvement where the child responds to the sensory challenges as a way of getting involved. For example, they may look at you when you block their path or put your hand on a spot on the rug they are touching. They may crave being squashed below pillows, or will hold your hand to jump up and down, or will remove Koosh balls touching their bodies.

Affect: They lack interpersonal warmth or pleasure and usually show flat or inappropriate unmodulated affect.

Communication and Language: These children evidence few, if any, consistent simple intentional gestures, except for sensation-seeking behaviors or food. They do not use expressive language, do not engage in symbolic play, and do not even seem preoccupied with certain objects.

Sensory Processing: These children show more self-stimulation and rhythmic behaviors than perseverative behavior with objects (as Pattern C does). They constantly seek sensory experiences through their bodies, using motion, touch, pressure, "looking", etc., but are unable to connect these experiences to interpersonal interactions and feelings. On the one hand, they tend to be under-reactive to sensation and have low motor tone, requiring more and more intense input to respond. On the other hand, they may be acutely sensitive to certain sensations, to which they over-react and want to avoid. Both under- and over-reactivity are typical, e.g., children are over-reactive to tactile and certain features of auditory input (hypersensitive to certain sounds), and under-reactive to vestibular and proprioceptive experiences, resulting in seeking (craving) these inputs from others as well as self-stimulation. These children also have the least sense of where their bodies are in space (often requiring intense physical activity to register feedback) and the most difficulty with motor planning (unable to sequence movements to manipulate toys, build, do puzzles, etc.). Sensation-seeking behaviors provide the openings for intentional communication and language.

Adaptation: These children tend either to show catastrophic reactions to new experiences or changes in familiar routines and environments with extreme tantrums or panic states, or to completely under-react, showing little or no responsiveness and "tuning out."

This pattern should not be diagnosed below five months of age, because while the capacity to relate and attend begins earlier, it may not be evident until five months, given individual variations.

With interventions that provide the necessary levels of sensory and affective involvement and deal with the under-reactivity, hypersensitivities and motor planning difficulties, these children may evidence gradually increasing relatedness and purposefulness.

Pattern B:

Relatedness and Interaction: The child is in and out of relatedness, appearing to quickly take flight from moments of connectedness. The child will briefly engage in an activity with another but not directly with the other person. For example, these children can be intermittently engaged via the obstruction of their repetitive activity (e.g. pushing a train back and forth, or blocking their path, or hiding the car they want, etc.).

Affect: Affect appears accessible but fleeting, with small islands of shallow satisfaction and pleasure but no deep interpersonal joy and pleasure. These children tend to enjoy repetitive or perseverative activity with objects (rather than only self-stimulation), but also depend on over-focusing on these objects to control and modulate other sensory and interpersonal input (see below).

Communication and Language: These children can intermittently use simple intentional gestures, including motor gestures, vocalization and affect cues, to interact around a mechanical activity, e.g., take a toy from you and throw it down repeatedly. Occasionally, constructive interactions are possible, such as handing them a block to build with, or adding a car to their line (as long as you do not change their "order"). At around one year, the child may begin to speak a few words such as "bye-bye," "bottle", "mom" or "dad", but then stops acquiring language and in fact begins to "lose" the language the child had between 15-24 months.

Sensory Processing: These children show more mixed patterns of sensory reactivity and motor tone. They are much more organized (than Pattern A) in their seeking of sensation, deliberately running, jumping, wanting to be in the swing, and seeking tactile input. They also show a greater sense of where their bodies are in space, not always stepping on or through things. Visual and spatial skills are often more developed than auditory processing, e.g. children may be able to do puzzles, or know what direction to walk in. Motor planning is still very difficult, but children can do simple or well-practiced sequences (e.g., go on slide) or play with toys that roll or have simple cause-and-effect actions.

Adaptation: These children do not tolerate changes and transitions well, but can adapt to routines if not overwhelmed by sensory overload. They remain very constricted in the range of experience they can deal with, including limits on what they will eat and wear.

This pattern should not be diagnosed until nine months of age because while the capacity for interactive sequences begins earlier, it may not be evident until nine months, given individual variations.

With interventions that extend interactive sequences, these children may evidence increasingly complex behavioral and affective interactions.

Pattern C:

Relatedness and Interaction: The child relates to others but still in an in-and-out way, and usually must be the one in control, both initiating and ending the interactions. The child can be wooed directly and through objects, but can get easily overloaded. If overloaded, the child will withdraw in an organized way, such as moving to the other side of the room, or hiding behind a chair, perhaps resuming eye contact when "safe." These children can be engaged in constructive interactions, building on their interests and favorite objects, such as hiding the car keys, or crashing trains with them. Such activities will often bring a smile. They also tend to be very perseverative and preoccupied with certain objects but will let you make the perseverative behavior interactive, e.g. they will somewhat playfully remove your hand from behind the door they keep trying to open and close repeatedly. They can be wooed into interaction and tolerate more "interference." The child has a sense of what he or she wants and makes some effort to help himself or herself. The child will tend to seek some boundaries, e.g. separating himself or herself from others by standing behind a bench to interact in a more organized manner.

Affect: There are islands of real interpersonal pleasure coupled with more organized avoidance and times of aloofness. Pleasure is evident in spontaneous interaction, very predictable gestural games and songs (nursery rhymes) which have been done repeatedly, and physical activities (e.g. rough-housing).

Communication and Language: These children are consistently capable of simple gestures and some islands of complex intentional communication to get needs and desires met, e.g., a child will take a parent's hand to help him open the door. These children may gradually learn to use some single words or two word phrases intentionally. In many cases this follows the disruption of spontaneous language (or simple sign language or pointing to pictures) acquisition between 18-24 months. These children more easily learn rote verbal patterns such as the alphabet, familiar nursery songs or video and book scripts. These children require lots of interaction to maintain progress in the intentional use of language, and with such practice become more spontaneous and adaptive.

These children may also use words "under fire" when their needs or wishes are being blocked and they feel intensely angry. This will usually be accompanied by some motor action. Children may also begin to experiment with simple symbolic play related to their direct experience, recognizing toys for what they are (e.g., may try to eat a toy cookie or get in a toy car, even sitting on a small school bus or toy horse).

Sensory processing: These children are beginning to integrate their sensations, but still show mixed reactivity with greater preponderance to over-react and get excitable. Motor planning is still difficult but more readily mastered (in contrast to the under-reactivity of Pattern A).

Adaptation: These children are the most adaptive of the three types, but new experiences are difficult. They tend to use organized negative intentional avoidance and only intermittently withdraw. They are better with transitions when given enough time and cues and gestures to prepare.

This pattern should not be diagnosed below 15 months of age because while the capacity for complex behaviors and gestures begins earlier, it may not be evident until 15 months of age, given individual variations. These children may at times become behaviorally (and later on verbally) fragmented and purposefully negative or avoidant (e.g., turning away) when overloaded. With interventions that prolong interactive sequences and foster symbolic elaboration of affects, these children may evidence continuous increases in their intimacy, emotional expressiveness, and level of symbolic thinking.

Appendix 3

Outline of Classification System

Guidelines to selecting the appropriate diagnosis

The primary diagnosis should reflect the most prominent features of the disorder. The following guidelines will assist the clinician in determining which diagnosis takes precedence.

1. Traumatic stress disorder should be considered as a first option, i.e., the disorder would not be present without that stress.

2. Regulatory disorders should be considered if there is a clear constitutionally- or maturational-based sensory, motor, processing, organizational, or integration difficulty.

3. Adjustment disorder diagnosis should be considered if the presenting problems are mild and of relatively short duration (less than four months), and associated with a clear environmental event.

4. Disorders of mood and affect should be considered where there is neither a clear constitutionally- or maturational-based vulnerability, nor a severe or significant stress or trauma, and when the difficulty is not mild or of short duration.

5. Multisystem developmental disorders and reactive attachment/deprivation/maltreatment disorder should take precedence over all other categories.

6. Relationship disorder should be considered where a particular difficulty occurs only in relationship to a particular person.

7. Do not use Axis I if the only difficulty involves the relationship.

8. Reactive attachment/deprivation/maltreatment disorder should be reserved for inadequate basic physical, psychological and emotional care.

9. Common symptoms such as feeding and sleep disorders require assessment of the underlying basis for these difficulties, e.g., acute trauma, adaptation reaction, or reactive attachment/deprivation/maltreatment disorder, regulatory and multisystem developmental disorders, or problems in their own

right.

10. On rare occasions, a child may have two primary conditions (e.g., a sleep disorder and a separation anxiety disorder).

Axis I: Primary Diagnosis

The primary diagnosis should reflect the most prominent features of the disorder.

100. Traumatic Stress Disorder

A continuum of symptoms related to a single event, a series of connected traumatic events, or chronic, enduring stress:

1. Re-experiencing of the trauma, as evidenced by:
    a. Post-traumatic play
    b. Recurrent recollections of the traumatic event outside play
    c. Repeated nightmares
    d. Distress at reminders of the trauma
    e. Flashbacks or dissociation

2. Numbing of responsiveness or interference with developmental momentum
    a. Increased social withdrawal
    b. Restricted range of affect
    c. Temporary loss of previously acquired developmental skills
    d. A decrease in play

3. Symptoms of increased arousal
    a. Night terrors
    b. Difficulty going to sleep
    c. Repeated night waking
    d. Significant attentional difficulties
    e. Hypervigilance
    f. Exaggerated startle response

4. Symptoms not present before
    a. Aggression toward peers, adults or animals
    b. Separation anxiety
    c. Fear of toileting alone
    d. Fear of the dark
    e. Other new fears
    f. Self-defeating behavior or masochistic provocativeness
    g. Sexual and aggressive behaviors

h. Other nonverbal reactions, e.g. somatic symptoms, motor reenactments, skin stigmata, pain, or posturing

200. Disorders of Affect

Focuses on the infant's experience and on symptoms which are a general feature of the child's functioning rather than specific to a situation or relationship

201. Anxiety Disorders of Infancy and Early Childhood

Levels of anxiety or fear, beyond expectable reactions to normal developmental challenges

1. Multiple or specific fears

2. Excessive separation or stranger anxiety

3. Excessive anxiety or panic without clear precipitant

4. Excessive inhibition or constriction of behavior

5. Lack of development of basic ego functions

6. Agitation, uncontrollable crying or screaming, sleeping and eating disturbances, recklessness, and other behaviors

Criterion: Should persist for at least two weeks and interfere with appropriate functioning

202. Mood Disorder: Prolonged Bereavement/Grief Reaction

1. The child may cry, call, and search for the absent parent, refusing comfort.

2. Emotional withdrawal, with lethargy, sad facial expression, and lack of interest in age-appropriate activities.

3. Eating and sleeping may be disrupted.

4. Regression in developmental milestones.

5. Constricted affective range.

6. Detachment.

7. Sensitivity to any reminder of the caregiver.

203. Mood Disorder: Depression of Infancy and Early Childhood

Pattern of depressed or irritable mood with diminished interest and/or pleasure in developmentally appropriate activities, diminished capacity to protest, excessive whining, and diminished social interactions and initiative. Disturbances in sleep or eating.

Criterion: At least two weeks.

204. Mixed Disorder of Emotional Expressiveness

Ongoing difficulty expressing developmentally appropriate emotions.

1. The absence or near absence of one or more specific types of affects
2. Constricted range of emotional expression
3. Disturbed intensity
4. Reversal of affect or inappropriate affect

205. Childhood Gender Identity Disorder

Becomes manifest during the sensitive period of gender identity development (between approximately 2-4 years)

1. A strong and persistent cross-gender identification

   a. Repeatedly stated desire to be, or insistence that he or she is the opposite sex

   b. In boys, preference for cross-dressing or simulating female attire; in girls, insistence on wearing stereotypical masculine clothing

   c. Strong and persistent preferences for cross-sex roles in fantasy play or persistent fantasies of being the opposite sex

   d. Intense desire to participate in the games and pastimes of the opposite sex

   e. Strong preference for playmates of the opposite sex

2. Persistent discomfort with one's assigned sex or sense of inappropriateness in that gender role
3. Absence of nonpsychiatric medical condition

206. Reactive Attachment Deprivation/Maltreatment Disorder of Infancy

1. Persistent parental neglect or abuse of a physical or psychological nature, undermines the child's basic sense of security and attachment;
2. Frequent changes in, or the inconsistent availability of, the primary caregiver; or
3. Other environmental compromises which prevent stable attachments.

300. Adjustment Disorder

Mild, transient situational disturbances related to a clear environmental event and lasting no longer than four months

400. Regulatory Disorders

Difficulties in regulating physiological, sensory, attentional, motor or affective processes, and in organizing a calm, alert, or affectively positive state. Observe at least one sensory, sensory-motor, or processing difficulty from the list below, in addition to behavioral symptoms.

1. Over- or under-reactivity to loud or high- or low-pitched noises.

2. Over- or under-reactivity to bright lights or new and striking visual images.

3. Tactile defensiveness and/or oral hypersensitivity.

4. Oral-motor difficulties or incoordination influenced by poor muscle tone and oral tactile hypersensitivity.

5. Under-reactivity to touch or pain.

6. Gravitational insecurity.

7. Under- or over-reactivity to odors.

8. Under- or over-reactivity to temperature.

9. Poor muscle tone and muscle stability.

10. Qualitative deficits in motor planning skills.

11. Qualitative deficits in ability to modulate motor activity.

12. Qualitative deficits in fine motor skills.

13. Qualitative deficits in auditory-verbal processing

14. Qualitative deficits in articulation capacities.

15. Qualitative deficits in visual-spatial processing capacities.

16. Qualitative deficits in capacity to attend and focus.

Types of Regulatory Disorders

401. Type I: Hypersensitive

Two characteristic patterns:

Fearful and Cautious:

Behavioral patterns -- excessive cautiousness, inhibition and/or fearfulness

Motor and sensory patterns -- over-reactivity to touch, loud noises, or bright lights

Negative and Defiant:

Behavioral patterns -- negativistic, stubborn, controlling, and defiant; difficulty in making transitions; prefers repetition to change

Motor and sensory patterns -- over-reactivity to touch and sound; intact visual-spatial capacities; compromised auditory processing capacity; good muscle tone and motor planning ability; show some delay in fine motor coordination

402.   TYPE II: Under-reactive

Withdrawn and Difficult to Engage:

Behavioral patterns -- seeming disinterest in relationships; limited exploratory activity or flexibility in play; appear apathetic, easily exhausted, and withdrawn

Motor and sensory patterns -- under-reactivity to sounds and movement in space; either over- or under-reactive to touch; intact visual-spatial processing capacities, but auditory-verbal processing difficulties; poor motor quality and motor planning

Self-Absorbed:

Behavioral patterns -- creative and imaginative, with a tendency to tune into his or her own sensations, thoughts, and emotions

Motor and sensory patterns -- decreased auditory-verbal processing capacities

403.   Type III: Motorically Disorganized, Impulsive

Mixed sensory reactivity and motor processing difficulties. Some appear more aggressive, fearless and destructive, while others appear more impulsive and fearful.

Behavior patterns -- high activity, seeking contact and stimulation through deep pressure; appears to lack caution

Motor and sensory patterns -- sensory under-reactivity and motor discharge

404.   Type IV: Other

500.   **Sleep Behavior Disorder**

Only presenting problem; under three years of age; no accompanying sensory reactivity or sensory processing difficulties. Have difficulty in initiating or maintaining sleep; may also have problems in calming themselves and dealing with transitions from one stage of arousal to another.

600.   **Eating Behavior Disorder**

Shows difficulties in establishing regular feeding patterns with adequate or appropriate food intake. Absence of general regulatory difficulties or interpersonal precipitants (e.g., separation, negativism, trauma).

700.   **Disorders of Relating and Communicating**

1.   DSM-IV conceptualization Pervasive Developmental Disorder or

2.   Multisystem Developmental Disorder

Multisystem Developmental Disorder:

1.   Significant impairment in, but not complete lack of, the ability to form and maintain an emotional and social relationship with a primary caregiver.

2.   Significant impairment in forming, maintaining, and/or developing communication.

3.   Significant dysfunction in auditory processing.

4.   Significant dysfunction in the processing of other sensations and in motor planning.

701.   Pattern A

These children are aimless and unrelated most of the time, with severe difficulty in motor planning, so that even simple intentional gestures are difficult.

702.   Pattern B

These children are intermittently related and capable some of the time of simple intentional gestures.

703.   Pattern C

These children evidence a more consistent sense of relatedness, even when they are avoidant or rigid.

Axis II: Relationship Classification

Three aspects of a relationship:

1.   Behavioral quality of the interaction

2.   Affective tone

3.   Psychological involvement

901.   Overinvolved relationship

Physical and/or psychological overinvolvement

1.   Parent interferes with infant's goals and desires

2.   Over-controls

3.   Makes developmentally inappropriate demands

4.   Infant appears diffuse, unfocused, and undifferentiated

4.   Displays submissive, overly compliant behaviors or, conversely, defiant behaviors

5.   May lack motor skills and/or language expressiveness

902. Underinvolved relationship

Sporadic or infrequent genuine involvement

1. Parent insensitive and/or unresponsive
2. Lack of consistency between expressed attitudes about infant and quality of actual interactions
3. Ignores, rejects, or fails to comfort
4. Does not reflect infant's internal feeling states
5. Does not adequately protect
6. Interactions under-regulated
7. Parent and infant appear to be disengaged
8. Infant appears physically and/or psychologically uncared for
9. Delayed or precocious in motor and language skills

903. Anxious/Tense relationship

Tense, constricted with little sense of relaxed enjoyment or mutuality

1. Overprotective and oversensitive
2. Awkward or tense handling
3. Some verbally/emotionally negative interactions
4. Poor temperamental fit
5. Infant very compliant or anxious

904. Angry/Hostile relationship

Harsh and abrupt, often lacking in emotional reciprocity

1. Parent insensitive to infant's cues
2. Handling is abrupt
3. Infant frightened, anxious, inhibited, impulsive, or diffusely aggressive
4. Defiant or resistant behavior
5. Demanding or aggressive behaviors
6. Fearful, vigilant, and avoidant behaviors
7. Tendency toward concrete behavior

905. Mixed relationship

Combination of the features described above

906. Abusive relationships

a. **Verbally abusive relationship**

1. Intended to severely belittle, blame, attack, overcontrol, and reject the infant or toddler

2. Reactions vary from constriction and vigilance to severe acting-out behaviors

b. **Physically abusive relationship**

1. Physically harms by slapping, spanking, hitting, pinching, biting, kicking, physical restraint, isolation

2. Denies food, medical care, and/or opportunity to rest

3. May include verbal/emotional abuse and/or sexual abuse

c. **Sexually abusive relationship**

1. Parent engages in sexually seductive and overstimulating behavior -- coercing or forcing child to touch parent sexually, accept sexual touching, or observe others' sexual behaviors

2. Young child may evidence sexually driven behaviors such as exhibiting himself or trying to look at or touch other children

3. May include verbal/emotional abuse and/or sexual abuse

Axis III: Medical and Developmental Diagnoses

Indicate any coexisting physical (including medical and neurological), mental health, and/or developmental disorders, using DSM IV, ICD-9,10, DSM PC, and specify OT, PT, special education, and other designations.

Axis IV: Psychosocial Stressors

Identify source of stress (e.g. abduction, adoption, loss of parent, natural disaster, parent illness, etc). Overall impact of stress:

Mild effects -- causes recognizable strain, tension or anxiety but does not interfere with infant's overall adaptation

Moderate effects -- derails child in areas of adaptation but not in core areas of relatedness and communication

Severe effects -- significant derailment in areas of adaptation

2. Severity (mild to catastrophic)

3. Duration (acute to enduring)

4. Overall impact (none, mild, moderate, severe)

Axis V: Functional Emotional Developmental Level

A. **Essential processes or capacities**:

1. Mutual attention: Ability of dyad to attend to one another

2. Mutual engagement: Joint emotional involvement

3. Interactive intentionality and reciprocity: Ability for cause and effect interaction; infant signals and responds purposefully

4. Representational/affective communication: Language and play communicate emotional themes

5. Representational elaboration: Pretend play and symbolic communication that go beyond basic needs and deal with more complex intentions, wishes, or feelings

6. Representational differentiation I: Pretend play and symbolic communication in which ideas are logically related; knows what is real and unreal

7. Representational differentiation II: Complex pretend play; three or more ideas logically connected and informed by concepts of causality, time and space

  B. Functional Emotional Developmental Level Summary

1. Has fully reached expected levels

2. At expected level but with constrictions -- not full range of affect; not at this level under stress; only with certain caregivers or with exceptional support

3. Not at expected level but has achieved all prior levels

4. Not at current expected level but some prior levels

5. Not mastered any prior levels

Appendices

  1. Parent-Infant Relationship Global Assessment Scale

Assesses the quality of the infant-parent relationship, ranging from well adapted (90) to grossly impaired (10)

  2. Multisystem Developmental Disorder

Detailed description of three pattern types

  3. Outline

Case Vignettes

Seventeen vignettes illustrate the application of the diagnostic profile. Each vignette includes a description of presenting problems, a discussion of the differential diagnosis, implications for intervention, and the diagnostic profile, using the five axes.

Case Vignettes

These cases were submitted by participants in the ZERO TO THREE/National Center for Clinical Infant Programs Diagnostic Classification Task Force, who work in a variety of settings. The children described could be treated in a variety of settings, including parent-infant centers, early intervention programs, developmental and infant mental health centers, child psychiatry service settings, and private practice. The discussions of intervention do not specify a type of setting, nor do they specify the involvement of professionals from particular disciplines. Instead they offer guidance on the issues which should be addressed by any intervenor working with this child and family.

The intervention described after each case is intended to illustrate one type of approach that might meet the individual needs of the child and family as described in the case material and summarized in the diagnostic profile headings. There are likely to be other approaches to these cases that might be of benefit. A more definitive discussion of therapeutic approaches for different problems will be presented in a future publication of the ZERO TO THREE Diagnostic Classification Task Force, which will present detailed case studies and treatment guidelines.

Case 1: Sally

Case Description:

Sally, 26 months, had evidenced a healthy pattern of physical, emotional, and cognitive development. Then she, her six-month-old brother, and their 32-year-old mother were stabbed multiple times by their father/husband during an acute paranoid psychotic episode. Following surgery Sally was hypervigilant, refused to go to sleep, and had nightmares once she did. She was reassured she would be safe and started to wake only occasionally, but could not report the content of her bad dreams. Through play it became clear she was quite confused about the event and who the actual perpetrator of the abuse had been.

When Sally was taken to see her mother in the hospital, she screamed, "No!" and demanded to return to her room. Sally was reassured and told exactly what had happened and where the family members were, but she continued to express and play out her confused experience. During subsequent sessions she would continue to confuse who had actually stabbed her: at various times it would be mother, therapist or a stranger. While her play was very stereotypical in acting out the traumatic event, she pursued it again and again and did not engage in other kinds of play. She became more withdrawn and subdued. Although her overall developmental abilities did not appear to diminish, Sally started to reject tasks she had previously completed with pleasure, claiming she could not do it any more or that it was too hard.

Discussion:

The diagnosis of psychic trauma disorder is self-evident. Sally was an attractive and bright little girl with a history of otherwise healthy development and relationships. One can only speculate as to the reasons for Sally's confusion. She may have felt her mother should have protected her in general, since mother was clearly her primary attachment figure, and at such a young age she did not have solid object constancy and differentiated role models. Nor could she comprehend her father as an aggressor, so unlike the person she knew before. While she immediately started to re-enact the trauma and her confusion, her overall affect and attitude did not change until it was apparent she could not solve what had happened and began to feel more and more helpless.

This diagnosis takes precedence over other possible difficulties which might become evident during treatment. These could be added if necessary.

Intervention:

Crisis intervention was immediately available to Sally and her mother and brother when they were hospitalized, but it is clear that the family should continue in therapy as long as necessary. That Sally appeared to be worsening made it clear that she needed play therapy together with her mother, who could learn symbolic play approaches to help Sally work through the trauma, especially with regard to the safe expression of anger and aggression in everyday life. Since dealing with anger and aggression coincides with the expectable developmental challenges of a 26-month-old, it is important that Sally receive support to work through the trauma now, so that its effects do not derail her emotional development, and to foster effective coping strategies. In addition, Sally's mother needs individual treatment, since discussion of her feelings in the presence of her children should be limited. The mother will also need counseling to address the children's difficulties at home, ways to help them regain their security, how to talk about the father, and what to do if and when he recovers.

Diagnostic Impression:

Axis I: Psychic Trauma Disorder
Axis II: Relationship Disorder - Father - Physically Abusive; Mother - none
Axis III: Physical Injury
Axis IV: Psychosocial Stress - Severe effects
Axis V: Functional Emotional Developmental Level - At expected level with constrictions

Case 2: Richard

Case Description:

Richard, almost four, was very much a "tyrant" at home, ordering his parents to do this and that, as he insisted on having his way with everything. At school, in contrast, he was a "pleasant and polite" child, who related well to other children. He would not engage in pretend play with his parents, but he did with friends. He had learned to exercise control over his bowel movements at 36 months after great struggles over wiping and smearing his feces. But after only two months of bowel control, he began soiling his pants, each time soiling a little, and going to the bathroom ten times a day. At the time this pattern of behavior began, Richard's younger brother was just beginning to crawl.

Mother felt that she and Richard had a warm, loving relationship even though he did not show a lot of affection or cuddling with her. He enjoyed rough and tumble play with his father. Richard had developed language well, but had been a late walker (at 18 months), was still not very well coordinated, and had slightly delayed fine motor skills. His parents also remembered having to work hard to encourage two-way communication, since Richard tended to be very passive. During his toddler years he again tended to be unassertive and negative, but he was able to engage in complex interactions. He was an early talker and could make his needs known, in terms of "give me that," but still used negativism and passive modes to deal with conflict and to "get even" with his parents.

Father felt he was very close to his son though mother handled the "day to day stuff." He was a warm person, who seemed tense and anxious but very committed to Richard. Mother was a sweet and warm person, but seemed very tense, particularly in the area of cleanliness and neatness; she recalled how the smell of feces had disgusted her as a child. Both parents seemed to realize that their own tensions and anxieties around this issue might be contributing to the difficulty.

Richard presented as a nice-looking, very calm, but tentative child. He talked in a rather passive way, but was clearly engaged, warm and trusting. His mood was even; he had good impulse control and good attention. However, he had a narrow range of affect, with not much intensity to his pleasure or anger. He set up dolls with "good guys" who were hugging, and "bad guys" who were fighting. He then transformed one bad guy into a monster that ate up all the other dolls. Out of this aggression there emerged a mother trying to find the baby doll. He then found a whale who was asleep on the roof of a house while some kids played inside. His play consisted of these little fragments of themes, two minutes here and two minutes there, without it being clear what would happen, except for some apparent danger which he could not elaborate. Later, he vacillated between themes of things being defective (a doll missing an arm and leg who wanted to jump) and themes of power and accomplishment (a rocket ship going to the moon). He also talked of being scared of the dark, especially at night, but could not elaborate. He talked about being angry at his parents when they get angry at him, and denied he "could not wait" or felt jealous of his brother. He said he was happy "eating dinner and dessert."

Discussion:

Richard's difficulties had contributions from the constitutional and maturational side that were evidenced in fine and gross motor and motor planning delays. While not regulatory difficulties, they did contribute to his feeling insecure about his body. These delays were also associated with his difficulty learning certain automatic functions, a difficulty that had become a source of anxiety. In addition, he had a tendency to deal with frustration through passivity and avoidance, rather than assertiveness and confronting the problem. This often happens when a child does not have as much confidence in assertion through his motor system.

His parents were engaged and involved, but had some trouble fostering assertiveness and self-sufficiency, and had inadvertently supported his passivity by taking charge for him. Neither the constitutional-maturational delays or parental-environmental contributions were severe enough to derail his progression through his early emotional milestones, but he was not supported in symbolizing the aggressive and assertive side of life. In fact, his pretend play was a bit fragmented, rather than in a cohesive, assertive organization. Compounding this was mother's acute anxiety and intrusiveness about bowel training and fecal odors, and father's difficulty in getting involved in this task. The symptom of repetitive small bowel movements, with interest in smearing and smelling, was representative of both his passive and avoidant responsive to his parents and difficulty with acting out his assertiveness.

Richard's anxiety, manifest in his passivity, avoidance, tyrannical behavior and persistent difficulties with bowel movements, interfered with appropriate functioning and resulted in constricted affect.

Intervention:

Richard has good symbolic abilities but needs to learn to elaborate his fantasies, thoughts, and feelings with the support of a therapeutic relationship. Individual play psychotherapy, which includes his parents in the sessions, would help the family find safe and acceptable ways to deal with the more aggressive side of life and give more direct symbolic expression to their conflicts. These efforts could carry over into ongoing developmentally facilitating play and conversation as Richard grows.

Therapy would also support the family members' ability to reflect on their feelings. Collateral work with the parents would be essential, to differentiate their conflicts and projections, to support their parental roles, and to identify ways to support Richard, including limit setting. In addition, an occupational therapy assessment is indicted to determine the significance of

Richard's sensory-motor and motor difficulties, and to suggest a home program, with consultation or therapy as appropriate, to support sensory and motor aspects of Richard's development.

Diagnostic Impression:

Axis I: Anxiety Disorder
Axis II: While the relationship is perturbed in certain areas, it is not so severe or pervasive to constitute a disorder.
Axis III: None
Axis IV: Psychosocial Stress— Mild effects
Axis V: Functional Emotional Developmental Level — At expected representational level with constrictions

Case 3: Ben

Case Description:

Ben's nursery school teacher called again. Ben continued to hit and bite and the children were frightened of him. He was only calm in the paint corner, where he worked by himself and created wonderful, colorful images he could describe in detail even at age two. Ben's parents perceived their first child as "just fine" until nursery school. He started school shortly after his sister was born, and perhaps this contributed to his outbursts of aggression. As she became more active, so did he, directing his frustration and anger at her by pushing, knocking her over and even biting. Other children were afraid to play with him. With his parents, Ben could recite all the rules of acceptable behavior and say what he would do "next time," but in reality he was impulsive and appeared unremorseful, making others feel anxious and angry. Lots of "sorry's" and "time outs" later, Ben's parents sought help.

When first seen for evaluation, this cute, blond three-year-old boy appeared terribly anxious. He was clearly very bright, but also intense. Ben was curious and asked lots of questions about the toys, trying each out but not organizing any themes. With more support from the examiner, he could elaborate with the doctor kit, cutting off the doll's hurt foot. He then noticed the animals and reported, "The zebra is angry and bites because the mother and father hit." He proceeded to line up all the biting animals in one place and the "good" animals in another.

Ben could easily elaborate representationally. His characters were always angry, hitting, retaliating, and "in trouble" unless they could be alone. Ben usually responded to questions related to his play, but did not interact spontaneously, missing cues and gestures unless they were verbalized. He would have alligators eating people and missiles exploding everywhere. This would alternate with picking safe little figures, such as the Berenstein bear family, which he used to reenact his real-life situations as he struggled to be good and find safety in a world fraught with danger and trouble. He was always anxious and could not convey any emotions related to warmth, closeness or dependency.

Considering Ben's actions more carefully suggested several possible underlying processing difficulties. Ben showed alarm when anyone came too close unexpectedly, but when he initiated physical contact he was comfortable; thus he could reach out to be cuddled in the early hours of the morning. Even with people he knew very well, if they made a casual friendly gesture toward him, he would pull back and ask them not to touch him. When he played with toy figures, he had to hold one in each hand and be the only one to move. If he were in the middle of an action and something was said, he appeared not to attend. He was sensitive to sounds around him, easily distracted, and slow to orient himself, as he anxiously tried to figure out what he heard. He had difficulty recognizing "personal space" and would poke, bump and seek inappropriate contact with other children. He was also small for his age, tended to toe-in, and had low motor tone and motor planning difficulties.

Mother reported that Ben had always been a poor sleeper and an erratic eater, had a short fuse, and was quick to scream. He hated being picked up high or sudden movements, but walked early (at 10 months) after a very brief crawling period. Once Ben was on his feet, his earlier difficulties were less apparent, and concerns were set aside. As Ben got into increasing difficulty, Mother found herself assuming an overprotective role, continuously trying to buffer the criticism and anger of others and rationalize his difficulties. Over and over again, she would patiently talk with Ben, who promised to be "good." Ben's difficulties frightened her, since they reminded her of her brother who had disabilities, and she tried to minimize these and placate everyone.

Father traveled a lot and appeared to withdraw more and more, in efforts to control his own anger and identification with Ben. When he and Ben did play, it was usually checkers and board games with strict rules, and Ben demonstrated precocious abilities. Both parents were aware that Ben reminded them of either themselves (father), or someone in their own family (mother's brother). The parents' own relationship suffered as Ben's difficulties escalated, but they did not engage in physical abuse, tending to withdraw or overcompensate.

Further observations (for example of Ben's difficulty manipulating two toy figures in different hands at the same time) suggested the possibility of motor planning and perceptual-motor difficulties. In addition, he had difficulty looking at his play objects when trying to coordinate them, and related to this, had difficulty judging space and distance and tracking movement. These difficulties resulted in tremendous stress, since Ben received conflicting messages from his two eyes. He could not use vision efficiently to direct his movements or to correctly interpret other people's actions. He also showed reduced motor tone and tactile defensiveness. Ben's adaptation to the outside world was fragile. He dealt with uncertainty by being overly aggressive.

Discussion:

Ben presented with impulsive and aggressive behaviors typical of behavioral and conduct disorders. He was angry at the world which continuously criticized him, and depended on his protective mother for more and more "chances" to do better. Having become quite anxious in social situations, he was resorting to attacking first, before he was attacked. By age three, his emerging self-image was one of a bad, angry boy with no friends. While the interactive patterns with his family were becoming more perturbed, they did not appear to be causing his difficulties. As he had to function more and more in the outside world, which impinged on him unpredictably, he became increasingly reactive. Given the constitutional-maturational regulatory difficulties he had evidenced since birth, Ben could not tolerate the increasing sensory input as well as the emotional stress that accrued with the birth of his sister and social difficulties at school. Anxiety and behavioral problems resulted.

Intervention:

Ben may benefit from both play therapy and occupational therapy with a sensory integration focus to help with his significant sensory defensiveness and motor planning difficulties. A developmental vision exam is also indicated to assess the specific visual immaturities or problems that are contributing to Ben's difficulties, particularly in negotiating appropriate space and movement. In play therapy, Ben would learn safe ways to express himself symbolically and problem solving strategies to deal with the challenges he experienced. Therapy would also support more reflection and self-awareness. In Ben's case, ongoing play therapy may be needed to give him the consistent and sustained support he needs as he matures during the preschool years and responds to the treatment of the underlying processing difficulties that are contributing to his behavior.

Including the parents in the sessions would support learning symbolic expression and giving Ben the "power and control" he wanted in a safe way, as he came to grips with reality and the world's expectations. Parent counselling would be crucial, both to deal with Ben's behavioral difficulties and intense jealousy, as well as to work through the parents' feelings of guilt, anger, disappointment, and fear. Finally — but very importantly — ongoing consultation with Ben's teachers is crucial, since Ben's behavior could easily be seen as "just bad" or as representing the parents' failure to set appropriate limits. Such consultation would help Ben's teachers understand his strengths as well as specific difficulties and develop strategies to use at school to prevent conflicts and support his self-esteem.

Diagnostic Impression:

Axis I: Regulatory Disorder - Type III

Axis II: Overinvolved tendency (mother did not show this pattern with second child)

Axis III: None

Axis IV: Psychosocial Stress - mild effect

Axis V: Functional Emotional Developmental Level - Expected level with constrictions in range of affect and under stress

Case 4: Robert

Case Description:

Robert, a 16-month-old toddler, was referred for evaluation because of food refusal and failure to thrive. He was the first child of professional parents who underwent years of fertility treatment before he was conceived. He was born full-term, without any pre-, peri- or postnatal complications. Mother was home for two months and returned to work on a reduced schedule of 30 hours after finding someone to care for Robert at home. From birth he was an alert and curious baby, but showed little interest in feeding. However, in spite of drinking only 3-4 ounces of milk at a time, he grew well (at the 25th percentiles for height and weight) until nine months of age. Motor development was average; he sat at six months, crawled at nine months and walked independently at 13 months. He started to say words at nine months and had a vocabulary of 50 words at the time of the evaluation.

Around eight months of age, he started to refuse to open his mouth when spoonfed. Initially he could be distracted and opened his mouth unawares, but as he got older he tried to get out of the high chair, and would scream and throw the food and utensils when he could not get his way. An attempt was made to feed him as he ran around the room or sat on someone's lap. In spite of all the coaxing, distracting, and cajoling, Robert's food intake was poor; his milk bottles remained the major source of his caloric intake. By the time of the evaluation he had fallen below the fifth percentiles for weight and height.

Observations of feeding and play revealed interesting patterns. Initially he protested when he was put in the high chair but settled down for his mother and child care provider. However, when his father placed him in the high chair, Robert increased the intensity of his crying until his father took him out and put him on his lap. With each feeder he showed little interest in eating. After a few bites he would emphatically say "out" or "down." Immediately, the father would let him down and let him run around the room. His mother increased the intensity of her distractions and encouragement until he started crying "out," "out." She then took him out and tried to feed him on the run. The child care provider remained calm and told Robert, "No, you have to stay in the high chair." He started to cry, but she remained quiet and waited. In the midst of crying Robert looked at her, apparently to assess her reaction to his distress. When she smiled at him, he ceased crying, and a little later resumed feeding himself finger food from his tray.

Robert's behavior reflected what occurred at home. He ate most successfully for the child care provider, ate a little for his mother, but only wanted to interact with his father without eating. Robert's play interactions were delightful with all three. On the Bayley Scales Robert attained a developmental index of 125 and a motor index of 105. He had been a curious, engaging, and interpersonally sensitive boy from the beginning, with strong will and determination becoming increasingly evident in the last few months.

The exploration of the parents' upbringing and its effect on their own development revealed that the maternal grandmother suffered from bouts of psychotic depression. The grandmother's illness had been a great burden throughout the mother's childhood, although her father was supportive and helped the mother cope with the disruptions in their family life. The father came from a stable middle class family, but he experienced his parents as harsh and lacking warmth. Robert's parents had a strong marital relationship; they were understanding and supportive of each other. They both were very sensitive and realized that because of their own childhood experiences, they wanted to be very nurturing to their son, and found it difficult to say "no" and to set limits for him. The parents also felt that the years of yearning for a child had predisposed them to react with more anxiety when Robert refused to eat.

Discussion:

Robert is a bright, interpersonally sensitive, and strong-willed little boy who from birth appeared very interested in the external world and showed little awareness of his internal hunger cues. This lack of awareness became problematic when he was eight months old. His curiosity and wish for exploration of the environment became intensified, and he learned to control his caretakers by protesting being put or staying in the high chair. As he matured rapidly in his cognitive development, he increasingly exercised control and asserted his autonomy by refusing to eat. Because his parents became increasingly anxious about his poor food intake, they engaged in maladaptive interactional patterns of coaxing, cajoling and distracting him during feeding. This led to further external regulation of Robert's eating, and perpetuated his inability to recognize physiological feelings of hunger and to differentiate them from his wish for attention and control. Consequently, Robert failed to develop somatopsychological differentiation, a failure which led to inadequate food intake. All other aspects of Robert's development, including the regulation of sleep, were age-appropriate or precocious.

Intervention:

The evaluation process itself highlighted the maladaptive interactional patterns which had evolved as Robert moved into the second year of life and which would be the basis for developing an eating program which would be more consistent and relevant to learning to recognize his own hunger. In addition, consultation with the parents is needed on the larger emotional and developmental issues. To support the new guidelines and limits they would need to use, the parents will need to increase their engagement with Robert through play and other interactions. They would also need to learn how to shift from power struggles to support for creative use of imagination and symbolic expression of feelings. This would help Robert enter the symbolic world, where he could develop better behavioral organization and self-regulation.

Diagnostic Impression:

Axis I: Eating Behavior Disorder
Axis II: No Relationship Disorder
Axis III: None
Axis IV: Psychosocial Stressor - Mild effects
Axis V: Functional Emotional Developmental level - Has fully reached expected levels

Case 5: Alex

Case Description:

Alex, a nine-month-old (corrected for prematurity, eight-month-old) white infant was referred by Neurology for an evaluation after his eleventh hospitalization for alleged apneic bradycardia episodes and seizures. He is also being treated for chronic otitis media and gastroesophageal reflux. He is on phenobarbital and remains on a monitor because of mother's fears, despite medical recommendation to discontinue monitoring. Alex lives with his mother, age 32, and an older sister (9) and brother (8). He has been hospitalized an average of once a month since birth, due to shaking, staring spells, and "going limp" (despite his taking phenobarbital maintained at adequate levels). The child has had multiple EEGs, video EEGs, and urinary metabolic acid screens, with no findings. In addition, no health care professional has been a witness to these seizures. Mother reports that the seizures have been witnessed by the patient's friends and siblings. Mother states that they occur at various times during the day and that he even required CPR.

Alex was a product of rape. This circumstance plays a major factor in the mother's relationship with him. Early in the pregnancy, Alex's mother attributed her amenorrhea to the stress of post-rape anxiety, but then she discovered that she was three months pregnant. She candidly stated that she strongly considered abortion, but "My children convinced me to keep the baby." She described much ambivalence about this child. She was particularly concerned about the possibility of his being a biracial child, saying, "Since I couldn't see the rapist, I didn't know if he was black, white, Hispanic, or what." Alex's health was her other concern.

Mother stated that he was a happy baby. She felt she loved him more than her other children because she had more time to spend with him than she had had with her with her two older children, who were only a year apart. She stated that he would be a "normal" child if it were not for his medical problems. In addition, on an intake form, she stated that "Alex is life after rape."

Mother reports that she had had one ectopic pregnancy, nine miscarriages, and had borne three living children and one child who died after six weeks of life, secondary to a respiratory problem. She said that all of her pregnancies were complicated by premature births. During her pregnancy with Alex, she began to receive regular prenatal care at three months; she denied any alcohol or tobacco use. She took only phenobarbital, for tonic-clonic seizures which started after a car accident at 17. She reported being in another motor vehicle accident at five and one-half months gestation with this pregnancy. While not sustaining any serious injury, mother reports that the steering wheel was "imbedded in my uterus." She reports that sequelae to the accident included a partially ruptured placenta and preterm labor, controlled with hospitalization and medication. Alex was born at 36 weeks gestation by Cesarean section, without postnatal complications; Apgars were not known.

Mother felt that she had poor support from her family both during her pregnancy and after Alex's birth. She primarily attributes this to his being the product of a rape. Even after family members found out that he was not biracial, it was not until he was two to three months old, when he had his first "really bad seizure," that the family fully accepted him. Up until that time his name could not be mentioned in front of extended family members. The children helped name Alex. He was given the same middle name as the first name of the brother who had died in infancy.

Mother reports that Alex was fine until four weeks of age when, during a bath, he had his first seizure and became apneic. She expressed concern that she may have gotten water in his face or that he slipped underwater, although she repeatedly stated that she did not remember that happening. She also stated, "You know it only takes a few drops of water to drown a baby." (Hospital records report no fluid in his lungs following this initial episode.) Records document that he had a normal physical examination except that he had some slowing of the heart rate and a few apneic spells and was placed on a monitor.

Mother's additional concerns are in the areas of feeding, sleeping, and separation. She reports that Alex has difficulty swallowing and she has difficulty getting him to take solid foods. She also expressed fear that he might choke to death. (In a prior evaluation, an occupational therapist encouraged the mother to give him solid foods, but she did not follow these recommendations.) She reports, in addition, that he does not sleep for longer than two hours at a time. Mother's third concern is that "Alex cannot stand to be alone. He wants to be by my side at all times." She also said, "No one else can hold him." Mother says she cannot leave Alex because a caretaker would not know CPR.

Mother was very anxious as she repeated her concerns about Alex again and again. Unable to see her well-developed baby's assets and strengths, she projected her own fears of being damaged and vulnerable onto him. When she was asked to talk about her own feelings, she denied concerns about herself and quickly refocused on Alex.

Observations of mother and Alex at 9 months revealed an attractive, well-nourished and engaging child interacting in a warm and reciprocal manner. Mother and child seemed to mold very well, and Alex clearly responded to his mother's voice and facial expressions. He was also attentive to the environment and eager to explore it, despite being attached to the monitor. On a second visit, Alex's mother did disconnect the monitor, giving him a little bit more freedom. However, when Alex was not being restrained by a mechanical device, she made sure she kept him in close range. Though Alex clearly indicated he wanted to move about and explore, these cues were ignored by his mother; however, Alex did not protest when his mother redirected him to her. He responded to his mother with good eye contact, smiling, cuddling, and cooing, and did not appear anxious or clingy. In fact, he appeared to respond to everything she required. For example, during the session she frequently breastfed him for approximately five minutes on each breast. Alex did not fuss when he was removed from the breast while nursing and did appear eager to eat each time, though he did not signal for more. Alex did not appear anxious when the mother left during a separation/reunion task. He was quite engaging with the examiner and upon his mother's return, gave coos and smiles, good eye contact, and movement toward her.

Physical exam revealed bruises on the right forehead and just below the left eye. Mother reports that during one of Alex's spells, he fell and hit and bruised his head. Physical findings were consistent with the mother's story, but there was concern about possible abuse. Evaluation by the developmental pediatrician and testing (Bayley, Peabody, and Vineland) revealed age-appropriate motor, cognitive and preverbal functioning. Though mother was very concerned about Alex's feeding behavior, the occupational therapist found that he actively opened and closed his mouth, was able to manipulate the food to the back of his mouth, and swallowed without difficulty or choking.

Discussion:

The major concern here is the relationship between this child and mother and her ongoing ambivalence around his birth. His reported medical history is significant, but its validity is questionable. Despite mother's dramatic history, clinical observation and developmental assessments revealed Alex's development to be proceeding in an age-appropriate manner. There is therefore no Axis I diagnosis.

There is, however, considerable suggestion of a relationship difficulty. On the surface, Alex's mother shows genuine care and love and expresses her wish for him to develop normally, but her fears and ambivalence certainly break through. This is seen in her statements about him and in the interactive patterns that have begun between the two of them, specifically overprotectiveness, particularly around feeding and separation. The mother appears to project onto Alex her own medical vulnerability and her own difficulty in separating. This is seen in her restricting his age-appropriate exploration of his surroundings as he becomes more mobile. She cannot see his strengths, and he has difficulty asserting himself. The mother's personality difficulties are also manifest in diffuse generational boundaries with Alex's older siblings. Alex's "illness" serves to diminish the mother's sense of shame around the child's conception and to reconnect her with her family.

Possible physical abuse, including Factitious Disorder by Proxy, should be investigated.

Intervention:

This dyad would benefit from attending a parent-infant program which would support more pleasure and successful interactive learning with other parents and infants. It would be important to have both group discussions and individual psychotherapy built into such a program, which would: 1) be accepting and supportive to the parent, on both concrete and psychological levels; 2) interrupt the mother's current isolation at home with her child; 3) provide recognition and nurturance to her as a parent; and 4) help her embrace her other children. Outreach might be necessary to engage the mother in such a program by first wooing her in, and then encouraging her participation and sharing with others, and finally developing the individual therapeutic relationship she will need for herself. Alex would enjoy the stimulation of a larger setting, where he would be freer to explore and play with other children and receive the support of other relationships, and where any difficulties could be monitored.

Diagnostic Impression:

Axis I: No diagnosis
Axis II: Overinvolved Relationship Disorder
Axis III: Seizures (by mother's history only), apneic bradycardia, reflux, chronic otitis media.
Axis IV: Psychosocial stress - Moderate effects
Axis V: Functional Emotional Developmental Level - at expected levels with mild constrictions

Case 6: Miguel

Case Description:

Miguel, 37 months old, was physically attacking his two-month-old sister. He attended a different day care setting each day of the week. In day care, he evidenced a lack of social involvement, with one setting reporting that he had begun strangling a three-year-old peer. Mother had noticed decreased social relatedness from the start of her last pregnancy, when Miguel also began to exhibit echolalic language. At the time she experienced a mild depression, not wanting to be too close or involved with Miguel. As the pregnancy progressed, Miguel became less communicative, less interactive and resistant to going to day care. When he started to hit his infant sister, his parents talked to him and locked him in his room for time out.

Miguel's mother's pregnancy was unremarkable except for a mild viral illness and a Cesarean section. He weighed almost 9 pounds at birth, with Apgars of 9 and 9. Miguel was breast fed until 6 months and described as an active, smiling and cuddly baby who slept and ate well the first two years of life. Developmental milestones were met. He interacted with peers.

The family moved from Mexico to California when Miguel was 18 months old. At 20 months he became very echolalic but then seemed to improve until age 30 months. The episode of his echolalia and his improvement might have been in response to the change in language due to the geographic move and his exposure to English. However, the echolalia increased following a second major family move and placement in day care. This suggested that the echolalia was responsive to general stress related to changes in routine. This is supported by the fact that at this point Miguel became increasingly irritable and easily frustrated, intolerant of changes in routine, often overreactive to the environment, and frenetically active. He stopped responding to questions, became extremely distressed when he had to separate from his parents, and withdrew from children except when he became excited or violent.

Evaluation indicated over-responsiveness and overstimulation to verbal and visual input. While he had age-level vocabulary, expressive language was echolalic and he tended to describe objects by function rather than labels. Miguel also appeared poorly coordinated and had motor planning problems. His play was stereotypical and repetitive, and interaction was difficult with adults and children. Nevertheless, he had some symbolic play capacities, which conveyed fragmented themes of separation, dependency, abandonment, and anger and aggression at his sister and peers. Miguel's parents found it very difficult to engage him and vacillated between impatient questioning and withdrawal.

Family history revealed that father was dyslexic and had difficulty focusing his attention. He had learned to tune out external stimuli and tended to be unresponsive to outside attempts to gain his attention. He described himself as tending to seek distance from interpersonal relationships. Mother described herself as a good student but a shy child and adolescent. Her family had a history of unipolar and bipolar depression, and she described herself as mildly depressed since her recent pregnancy.

Discussion:

Miguel had experienced several sources of stress during the last year. His family made two major moves, he was placed in five different day care settings, his sister was born, his mother was mildly depressed, and his father was distant and preoccupied with so many family and work changes. These all point to the significant impact of family and environmental factors, suggesting a disorder of affect (anxiety, attachment or depression). However, Miguel also evidenced significant difficulties with self-regulation and sensory processing, since he was both over and under-reactive to various stimuli and became aggressive and echolalic under stress.

Had Miguel just presented symptoms related to a disorder of affect without the constitutional-maturational processing difficulties, the former may have become the primary diagnosis. But his difficulties with auditory processing, sensory modulation, and motor control were sufficiently significant to consider multisystem developmental disorder with regulatory features or a severe regulatory disorder with mixed features. Both of these conditions would be reactive to extraordinary stress in his life. The degree to which his difficulties include problems in relationships and language and communication patterns would determine which diagnosis would be most appropriate. Often the initial response to intervention will provide further data on the most appropriate diagnosis.

Intervention:

In this case, an intervention plan was implemented quickly, and Miguel made rapid gains. Initial intensity was an important factor: Miguel and his parents met twice a week with a play therapist who guided the opening and closing of circles of communication and the elaboration of symbolic themes. In addition, the therapist recommended that Miguel play individually with each of his parents for at least one hour a day. Miguel evidenced improved relating and more appropriate functional language. The parents met with the therapist weekly to discuss the meanings of Miguel's behavior, their own feelings, day-to-day management (especially with regard to Miguel's relationship with his sister), and the other treatment modalities. Miguel was referred for speech therapy and occupational therapy, since he continued to evidence difficulty in modulating sensory inputs and in motor planning. (These difficulties were not, however, derailing his ability to relate and communicate.) Miguel's mother was supported in her decision to take an extended maternity leave, and Miguel was enrolled in a small neighborhood preschool, where he could make friends who would be available for informal play outside of school hours. The family met monthly with the entire treatment team (play therapist, speech/language therapist, and occupational therapist) to monitor progress and modify the treatment program as Miguel progressed.

Diagnostic Impression:

Axis I: Regulatory Disorder - Type IV Other
Axis II: Relationship Disorder - Underinvolved
Axis III: None
Axis IV: Psychosocial Stress - Moderate to severe effects
Axis V: Functional Emotional Developmental Level - Has not achieved current level and reached earlier levels with constrictions

Case 7: Sarah

Case description:

Sarah began child care at three months so that her mother could return to work part-time. Both parents had postponed having children to finish their professional training; Sarah was very much wanted and loved. Her parents chose a family home child care setting run by a middle-aged, grandmother-ly woman who cared for a small number of children under five. Sarah would be the only child under one year of age. Both parents adjusted their work schedules so that Sarah would spend the shortest possible amount of time each day in child care. Mother would drop her off and Father would pick her up. The first day, Father felt Sarah had a glazed facial expression and seemed quite somber. His initial response was that he was overreacting to her mood, as a result of his own guilt about the fact she was in child care.

Over the next several days, however, Father became convinced that Sarah was having a difficult adjustment to the child care setting. It seemed to take longer and longer for her to warm up after their return home. In the fol-lowing week, due to scheduling needs, Sarah's mother picked her up from child care and confirmed the observation that Sarah had a glazed look, seemed sad and depressed, was motorically inactive, and took several hours to smile at either parent. Their concern resulted in a consultation.

On her first visit Sarah appeared very withdrawn. She did not make eye contact with either her parent or the examiner, and was quite still. On her second visit, on a day she had not been to child care, Sarah appeared dra-matically different. She was active, smiling, very engaged, and developmen-tally appropriate. Both parents were active in initiating interaction with Sarah, almost to the point of being intrusive. The parents also described the onset of sleep disturbance and problems with feeding. They had expected these problems to be getting better after two weeks in child care, but instead they were getting worse.

A visit to the child setting confirmed Sarah's parents' observations. The other children were actively engaged in play, but Sarah was in her crib, lying passively and seemingly depressed and withdrawn. In discussion with the child care provider it became clear she relied on the infant's cues to guide her responses. She described Sarah as a very quiet child who seemed to eat well and spend most of the time in the crib or play pen. She did not see her as unhappy or depressed, but rather as a child who "needed time to herself." This was in sharp contrast to the toddlers, who were expressing their wants and needs.

Discussion:

There were difficulties in the "match" between Sarah's experience with very attentive and stimulating parents and an equally warm, but less interactive child care provider. Sarah was also away from her parents for most of the day, and in a new setting. Thus she was experiencing both separation and less-than-optimal caregiving. From a diagnostic point of view, Sarah evidenced an adjustment disorder, though her reaction became so severe so quickly that the developing symptoms suggest vulnerability to a disorder of affect (i.e., depressed mood).

Intervention:

Two intervention possibilities were considered: a more gradual transition to the mother's return to work and a change to a caregiver who was more inter-active and similar to the parents. Sarah's parents wanted first to see how Sarah would respond to a change in child care provider. When a younger child care provider who was more like the parents was brought into the home, Sarah resumed her affective availability and curious, assertive interac-tive style. Her symptoms abated over the next several weeks. The parents were encouraged to come in for follow-up consultations.

Diagnostic Impression:

Axis I: Adjustment Reaction
Axis II: None
Axis III: None
Axis IV: Psychosocial Stressors - Moderate effects
Axis V: Functional Emotional Developmental Level - At expected level with constrictions

Case 8: Max

Case Description:

Max ran into the room without even glancing at the examiner or noting his parents were behind him. He ran toward the window and started waving his hands excitedly, chanting the ABC in a high-pitched voice. When either mother or father approached, he slipped by them and ran to the other side of the room. Max did not respond to being called and if pursued he either ran away or started to climb onto the chairs or couches, always finding a way to turn away. Mother finally swept him up and swung him around as she sang a nursery rhyme. As she turned Max let his head fall back, but after a few moments struggled to get out of her arms and ran back to the window chanting the ABC in a sing-song manner as he continued to wave his arms and laugh and giggle for no apparent reason. Although he did not play with toys, he would line up blocks and other objects briefly before dispersing them quickly if anyone approached. When approached with symbolic play, he quickly turned away, jabbering to himself.

Max was a beautiful child with long curly locks, well built, who ate and slept well and always seemed exceptionally happy as he excitedly "whirled" around his world. He had just started nursery school after turning two years of age and his parents were called in by the teachers and urged to get an evaluation done. Although his parents and pediatrician had noted he was not yet talking, his gross motor milestones had been on target and he enjoyed good health with the exception of a few ear infections.

Max never climbed on the playground equipment, did not like being touched and stuck to holding hard plastic objects, though he had recently begun to walk around with a bar of soap. Puzzles and building blocks were of no interest. Neither did Max watch TV or videos except for brief glances as he ran around his home. He did not respond to any verbal directions but was usually cooperative when he could see what was going on. Max seemed so happy and energetic all the time and had not caused any significant disruption to the family's life, although his four-year-old brother had come to ignore him. Most everyone else had stepped back as he seemed to take care of himself. Max liked to be rocked for bedtime stories and his ability to recite the ABC and numbers were joyfully praised as his first "language." He enjoyed riding on his mother's or father's back when they roughhoused but would not look at them directly. His other needs were anticipated and he almost never asked for anything, though he would sometimes come over for a food treat or alphabet blocks. His parents were engaged in busy careers and community activities and were struggling to keep their own marriage going. Max's difficulties brought them together in certain ways but their mounting anxiety and neediness resulted in considerable tension and exacerbation of their own difficulties.

A series of evaluations was quickly undertaken, confirming multiple difficulties with sensory processing, as well as communication and relating.

Discussion:

Understanding Max's frenetic movement and flight from others, his preoccupation with the never-changing alphabet and lining up objects, and his difficulties communicating and relating requires consideration of the severity of his sensory processing difficulties and the behavioral patterns which had become established. He certainly looked his worst when evaluated in a strange and stressful situation, but his anxious parents reported similar behaviors at home. Although they always felt he showed affection as an infant, it was not apparent to them that he usually faced away as he let them rock and sing, or that he could not organize such gestures as pointing to what he wanted or climb up to get something, since they were so quick to get him everything. He also ate and slept well, developed well motorically, making it more difficult to recognize sensory processing deficits (auditory, vestibular, proprioceptive, and motor planning).

Max's severe difficulties with self-regulation and under and over-reactivity to sensations and feelings point to consideration of a regulatory disorder or a multisystem developmental disorder. Had his difficulties not included relating and communicating, a severe regulatory disorder would have been indicated. Because he could not relate and communicate in any consistent, sustained or age-appropriate manner, nor regulate and organize his sensory experiences, his diagnosis was Multisystem Developmental Disorder. His patterns are not consistent with a circumscribed delay or dysfunction in cognition because of the evident difficulties in relating and the individualized nature of his communication difficulties.

Intervention:

A child like Max requires a very intensive intervention program to support his development. The primary focus would be on engaging him in an interactive relationship in which he would learn to communicate with others. In this case, therapy three times a week with his parents and nanny provided the base for the program. In this relationship-oriented therapy, Max's caregivers learned how to follow his lead, foster engagement, exchange affective and motor gestures, open and close circles of communication, and develop the symbolic world. This same interactive approach was then carried out on a daily basis at home, for a minimum of three hours a day. Speech and occupational therapies were started, each for two to three sessions per week. An elimination diet was begun to see if Max would respond to the elimination of certain foods from his diet. Max was also enrolled in a small preschool, which he attended three times a week with an aide, who helped him to interact with other children. This experience helped him learn in an environment full of children who **could** play and interact, and therefore could reach out to him, as well as be good role models. In addition, Max's parents met regularly with the therapist to discuss their experiences, the impact on the family and marriage, and day-to-day questions. Team meetings were held monthly with the parents to monitor progress and integrate the treatment efforts.

Diagnostic Impression:

Axis I: Multisystem Developmental Disorder

Axis II: No Relationship Classification

Axis III: None

Axis IV: Psychosocial Stressors - None

Axis V: Functional Emotional Developmental Level - Has not achieved current or prior levels

Case 9: Jimmy

Case Description:

"He doesn't look at me, he cries whenever I touch him or hold him, there's something wrong with him or something wrong with me." These were the first words expressed by the mother of four-month-old Jimmy. She felt he related better to his father and did not cry with him, but there was still no pleasure, enthusiasm, smiles, or positive emotion. Jimmy had given his nanny occasional faint pleasurable looks and perhaps a smile or two. Mother held him stiffly and looked anxious and worried. Her vocalizations were in a whispering, depressive-like monotone, followed by long silences. The baby looked past her with an expressionless, vague quality and began crying and twisting after ten minutes. There were no looks, smiles, frowns, or motor gestures, only an indifferent, flat, vague stare.

The history revealed an unremarkable pregnancy and delivery. As a newborn, Jimmy had good motor control and was able to be both alert and calm, responding to sights and sounds as well as touch and movement in the first weeks after birth. By the second month, Mother noticed he became less responsive — "He learned to hate me." Mother had a history of chronic depression beginning in late adolescence and had been treated with medications, ECT, and psychotherapy over the years. She had become an accountant and worked long days. Father was also a busy accountant and presented as a person who liked things done in an orderly fashion, on time, and on his schedule. He was frustrated that his son was "hard to warm up." He also wanted his wife to be a "better mother." He would not go into detail about how she disappointed him or about his own background.

The examiner was able to catch the baby's attention fleetingly, and elicited a faint look and quick smile, suggesting a sense of relatedness and connection. Jimmy appeared sensitive to high-pitched noises, loud noises, and overly animated facial expressions. His motor planning and muscle tone seemed fine, and he enjoyed robust movement in space. It was hard to assess visual-spatial or auditory processing as his looks and engagement were so fleeting. Jimmy showed the same fleeting engagement with his nanny. As the clinician worked with Jimmy, his attention and sense of engagement increased a little, suggesting that persistent wooing could have a positive effort.

Discussion:

The parent-family components, i.e., the mother's depression and the interactive component, are primary contributing components. The infant also presented constitutional and maturational patterns which made it more and more difficult to pull him into a greater sense of relatedness as time went on, though he did fairly well in the beginning, before the parent and interactive components began to impinge on his development. Since he presented with a clear pattern of depressed and irritable mood, with diminished interest and pleasure in the human world, and the interaction with his caregiver evidenced a number of challenges, a primary diagnosis of depression seems indicated.

Intervention:

The primary diagnosis would direct the intervention to interactive work before addressing the developmental delays with occupational and speech/language therapy. The regulatory component (hypersensitivities) would need to be taken into account in the intervention in order to woo this child into a fuller sense of engagement. In working with this infant and family, the clinician needs to give the infant help in focusing his attention as he is reengaged emotionally. Work with the mother would help her read his cues and recognize emotional signalling, which would help mother and infant rebuild their relationship. The intervention could be provided in an infant center, through home visits, or in a traditional office setting, but should involve both parents and the nanny. The clinician would need to understand the regulatory as well as the emotional components of Jimmy's situation in order to help him get "back on track."

Diagnostic Impression:

Axis I: Affect Disorder - Depression
Axis II: Underinvolved Relationship
Axis III: Monitor Sensory Processing
Axis IV: Psychosocial Stress - Severe effects
Axis V: Functional Emotional Developmental Level - Has not achieved expected levels (mutual attention and engagement

Case 10: Mark

Case Description:

Mark was an easy, undemanding baby who would smile and respond if approached quietly, but who did not initiate or seek much contact. In a busy household with tense working parents and a very demanding three-year-old sister, it was not readily apparent how underreactive he was. At 18 months he brightened when his parents sang nursery rhymes and danced and moved with him, but left on his own, he would watch his little cars moving back and forth, spin little objects, and often rub a little toy back and forth across his belly. He was also very sensitive to sounds, reacting with alarm to sirens and unexpected motor noises, and had everyone speaking to him in a near whisper. Yet at the regular speaking voice level, he was hard to engage. When he could be engaged, Mark was related, warm, and clearly a bright child. Thus, while he responded to wooing, he tended to tune-out and get over-focused on his own activities, conveying a sense of fragility and constant apprehension about how the world would impinge on him.

Both parents were concerned and anxious about Mark's development, with father tending to anticipate every need and providing every protection, and mother more able to encourage increased assertiveness but sometimes depressed and inconsistent. Both parents had difficulty setting limits. Mark vacillated between two confusing caregiving patterns. The parents were also experiencing significant marital difficulties.

At thirty months, Mark appeared to understand what was said when he was listening, but his listening was inconsistent. Noisy and crowded restaurants or shopping malls were distressing, but he sought out vibrating noises. Mark appeared withdrawn and unfocused. Sensitive wooing and pursuit would engage him briefly, but then he would retreat into simple repetitive behaviors with his toys which kept the world away. Pleasure was only evident when strong sensory-motor actions (running, jumping, swinging, etc.) gave him a clearer sense of where his body was in space and allowed him to organize and become aware of his experience. Mark had always tended to scan his environment and then overfocus on something small in front of him. Further examination indicated his eyes did not converge very well and he employed fragmented visual skills such as fixation, locking in, and tuning out.

Language and symbolic gestures remained very simple, but Mark had acquired language and carried out symbolic acts with dolls. He especially responded to sources of anxiety, such as toys breaking, dolls getting hurt or falling, things getting lost or messy, etc. Mark could engage in simple conversations around these issues, but anxiety drove him to repetition. He also presented compulsive behaviors to stay safe, such as insisting on leaving the door open "just a crack!" He was "fearful dictator" who wanted everything done his way to control the impact of the environment, but at the same time he was frightened and did not want others to compete or get angry at him. He often did not "tune in" when talked to in a routine speaking voice but became fearful at hearing certain high or low-pitched sounds.

Discussion:

When seen at 30 months, Mark was becoming increasingly anxious and constricted, retreating more and more into a self-absorbed world. He was not particularly fearful or aggressive, but appeared to find safety in marching to his own drummer, cautious about the impact and demands of the outside world. While he developed language and adequate cognition, he was not attentive to other people's communications. Mark was hypersensitive to certain high-pitched and vibrating sounds, but underresponsive to other sounds. He was underresponsive to movement and had poor motor planning. He was also underresponsive visually and had become overfocused and repetitive. Although at this age he certainly presented affective and interactive difficulties, these appeared to have developed secondary to being so underreactive and difficult to arouse since birth.

Intervention:

Intervention for Mark needed to address both the processing and emotional difficulties — the former, to support Mark's abilities to take in and interpret the world around him more accurately and securely, and the latter to help develop his interaction and communication with others, as well as to expand his relatively limited gestural and symbolic abilities to engage with peers in age-appropriate ways. Because he was at a crucial stage of development with respect to social interaction and increasing expectations, intensive therapeutic work was indicated. To address the sensory processing difficulties, Mark was referred for occupational and speech therapies and for evaluation of visual motor capacities and auditory reactivity and processing. He and his parents were to work with a therapist to improve communication and symbolic skills, as well as to discuss day-to-day caregiving approaches. His parents would be worked with to learn how to inspire Mark to want to interact and reach out, and Mark would be pulled into a greater and greater range of emotional interactions in both his therapy and home program.

Mark was also to attend an early intervention program offering speech and language therapy three times a week and a regular preschool twice a week. It was also recommended strongly that the parents seek help for their personal difficulties to deal with their conflicts and different approaches to Mark. Resolving family difficulties was important in its own right and would also allow Mark to benefit from the other intervention efforts.

Diagnostic Impression:

Axis I: Regulatory Disorder - Underreactive Type II
Axis II: Overinvolved Relationship

Axis III: None
Axis IV: Psychosocial Stress - Severe effects
Axis V: Functional Emotional Developmental Level - Has not achieved current expected level

Case 11: Jasmine

Case Description:

Jasmine was a healthy, emotionally and developmentally age-appropriate 19-month-old when she witnessed her mother being assaulted and raped by an acquaintance. After Jasmine's mother fought with the man for several minutes, he grabbed Jasmine and held a gun to her head in order to get her mother to obey his commands. Jasmine was not physically injured during the attack.

Immediately after the rape, mother and daughter moved a short distance away to live with a relative. Several weeks later, they moved back into the apartment where the rape had occurred, and Jasmine became obviously symptomatic. Immediately on returning to the apartment, she exhibited great distress and remained quite fearful until her mother rearranged the furniture. Afterwards, she was somewhat calmer, but she displayed a number of persistent symptoms.

Her sleep was quite disturbed. Although she would fall asleep without protest, she cried out three to four times per night, unresponsive and inconsolable until she fell back asleep again. She would also wake up screaming for her mother, or screaming at her mother's assailant to leave her alone. At these times, Jasmine could be comforted, although it took some time before she fell asleep again. On at least three occasions following the rape, she slept through the entire day without awakening, although in general Jasmine did not appear to her mother to be more tired than usual.

After the rape, aggressive behavior dominated Jasmine's interactions with younger children, although aggressive behavior had not been apparent before the rape. At the same time, Jasmine tended to avoid interacting with older children. She was noted to be more stubborn and defiant with her mother, but also to be more sensitive, and to cry more readily than before the rape. She became "more attached" to her pacifier after the trauma. After the rape, Jasmine tended to avoid contact with men, except for her mother's boyfriend. Once when her mother and the boyfriend were playfully wrestling together, Jasmine came over to him, hit him, and cursed him. Jasmine also developed staring spells that lasted for two to three minutes and occurred about two or three times per week. Her mother was unaware of any obvious precipitant for these episodes. During the spells, Jasmine was mute and unresponsive; she tended to "stare" without any seeming focus or recognition.

In her play, Jasmine developed a repetitive sequence in which she threw dolls down on the floor and hit them. She tended to repeat this over and over, without elaboration and without obvious affect, according to her mother. She did not demonstrate this play in the examiner's office, but only at home with her mother.

Discussion:

The diagnosis of traumatic stress disorder is self-evident. This child presents many of the indications characteristic of this disorder.

Intervention:

Jasmine and her mother require play psychotherapy, which would involve both direct play and parent guidance to help Jasmine regain the security she lost as a result of the trauma. Since the child's language is just emerging, it would be important for the mother to learn how to use unstructured play to help her daughter establish a sense of security and gradually work through the trauma. The mother needs to learn how to be comfortable following the child's lead with whatever Jasmine expresses, including anger and aggression toward the mother. Therapy sessions might be frequent at first, to quickly help the mother learn to play with her daughter every day, to recognize the signals which would be likely to upset Jasmine in daily life, and to respond to them appropriately. The mother might also benefit from individual counseling. If Jasmine's "staring" spells persist, further neurological evaluation would be needed.

Diagnostic Impression:

Axis I: Traumatic Stress Disorder
Axis II: No Relationship Diagnosis
Axis III: None
Axis IV: Psychosocial Stressor - Severe effects
Axis V: Functional Emotional Developmental Level - Has reached expected levels.

Case 12: Julie

Case Description:

Julie finally falls asleep at her mother's breast as they both lie on the large mattress on the floor. It is after midnight and the previous hours were spent pacing, rocking, and finally nursing to sleep. Julie is 13 months old. Her crib was abandoned six or seven months ago when mother could no longer bear the persistent crying of her first, long-awaited baby. She seemed so helpless, so rag-doll, so needy, that even father's anger and dismay could not sway mother from trying her best to assure that her daughter felt she could be cared for and would not be abandoned to crying herself to sleep.

Everyone blamed the mother for overprotecting her child. Her pediatrician told her to "let the baby cry so she'll learn to go to sleep." Her husband accused her of rejection.

Julie was born after a planned, healthy pregnancy and delivery. She appeared alert and responsive, quick to look around. Her mother was quick to hold her so that the baby would feel secure and trusting that someone was always there for her. While Julie enjoyed being held when dressed, she was sensitive to light touch when stroked and did not like the initial contact with water when bathed. However, she seemed to adapt. She became vigilant to loud or sudden noises, quickly seeking their source. Frequent feedings and night wakings were expected and nursing became the way to calm her during early months of fussy and colicky behavior. Nevertheless, the first six months of life were a pleasure for all. It was not yet apparent her poor self-regulation with sleeping and eating patterns or her sensitivities or reactivity should be of concern. Her good looking, listening and vocal responsiveness became the sensory pathways through which she was also able to begin conveying her intentions. Early communication was rich and intense.

At about six months the family moved to a new house, Julie reacted to a DPT shot, and started waking more frequently. This continued over the next half year, and worsened whenever she got ill. Parents also noticed Julie was the last to sit among her peers in mother's parent group, and was not quite crawling at 10 months. Even at thirteen months her sitting was still not stable and mother recalled she was slow to hold her head up. It was not apparent to anyone this pattern indicated low motor tone and motor planning difficulties.

But Julie vocalized all the time, began using a few words by 12 months, and seemed to understand much of what was said to her, following simple directions and repeating the words. Although she certainly cried to protest, she would not throw objects lest she lose her balance and had few ways to express anger safely. Nor did she become attached to any transitional objects, preferring mother at her side day and night. Separation anxiety actually worsened early in the second year when the family housekeeper, whom she knew well, left.

Mother did not recognize how quick she was to move in on her baby, offering help before she needed it and leading her in activities. This was not done in an intrusive or controlling manner, but in a subdued and rather passive fashion with long pauses. She was an anxious parent who was worried about what to do next lest she make a mistake. A pattern developed where Julie also became passive and permitted herself to be controlled by mother's overtures and gestures, and mother who looked anxious and hesitant and then became overprotective. Father could encourage more assertiveness and activity, putting implicit demands on Julie to respond to him. He would tend to retreat, however, in response to his wife's anxiety and doubted himself, even though he kept insisting Julie be allowed to cry at night so that she finally learn to fall asleep.

Discussion:

At thirteen months Julie was already a bright verbal child, with strong attachments and relatedness, who appeared happy and responsive to those she knew. She was only beginning to crawl, still had difficulty keeping her body upright even for sitting where she would stretch her legs out, widely spaced, and fix her shoulders to stiffen her back in order to maintain her upright posture. She was also quite sensitive to touch and was hesitant to explore unknown objects or spaces. Most difficult was the fact Julie still could not fall asleep without her mother lying with her and would not be left with anyone.

A primary sleep disorder could be considered given the duration of this difficulty, but accompanying sensory processing difficulties give precedence to the regulatory patterns. Similarly, a primary diagnosis of separation anxiety does not take into account the significant regulatory difficulties. While parental-environmental difficulties contributed to the problem, they did not account for poor motor tone and sensory reactivity. The combination of difficulties needing to be addressed can be expressed in the multi-axial diagnosis. This case illustrates that when both regulatory features and caregiving-interaction pattern are prominent, the regulatory disorder diagnosis takes precedence and the caregiving-interaction patterns are expressed in Axis II in terms of the relationship diagnosis.

Intervention:

This family would require a number of elements in their program. The mother needs help in learning to follow her child's lead and work through the anxieties she is feeling about meeting her child's needs and keeping her secure, and the father needs help in getting more involved and closer to his daughter. Weekly joint play sessions with Julie would encourage assertiveness, and gestural and symbolic expression of a range of feelings. Psychotherapy with the parents would help them step back, define their boundaries (i.e., reduce their tendency to project), and regain their perspective on the family. Parent guidance would provide ongoing support for dealing with sleep and separation issues. Julie could benefit from occupational therapy to improve her poor motor tone and motor planning as well as a daily caregiving program to reduce her sensory defensiveness.

Diagnostic Impression:

Axis I: Regulatory Disorder - Hypersensitive - Type I

Axis II: Overinvolved Relationship

Axis III: None

Axis IV: Psychosocial Stressors - Mild effects

Axis V: Functional Emotional Developmental Level—At expected level with constrictions

Case 13: Colin

Case Description:

Colin is the 3 1/2 year-old son of an upper middle class couple; he was referred by his nursery school teacher for a psychiatric evaluation because he was unable to get along with other children. The extensiveness of his cross-gender preoccupations became evident to the consulting psychiatrist—they had not previously been a concern to his parents—and Colin was referred to a specialist for further evaluation.

Colin was eager to talk, was uninterested in toys, and despite being only 3 1/2 years of age behaved like a compliant adult consenting to be interviewed. Throughout the interview he seemed riveted to our faces as if he was intensely studying every expression. Of particular note was his expressed preoccupation with "ladies with angry eyes." He talked about how afraid he was of a girl in his class who had angry eyes and, with obvious emotional pressure informing the performance, he proceeded to imitate her for us. In studying the family's home video tapes, we also discovered that he would make the same "angry eyes" while standing cross-dressed in front of a mirror.

During evaluation he said he hated being a boy and emphatically stated that he was born a girl and that "if you wore girls' clothes you could *really* become a girl." There was no evidence of anatomic dysphoria. Emotionally, he described himself as being more of a sad boy than a happy boy and as being lonely. He said that none of the other children liked him. He often worried about his parents when he was in nursery school. Intellectually, he was functioning in the very superior range according to standardized intelligence tests and there was no evidence of learning disabilities.

Colin's birth had been uneventful. His mother described him as an easy baby who would just "drink in" the world around him. Indeed, according to the mother, so satisfying was their early relationship that when Colin was weaned at age eight months — he had begun to bite his mother's nipples — she felt that while he might be ready to stop nursing, **she** was not. The father, meanwhile, felt excluded from the mother-infant bond, and even at the time of the referral felt he did not know how to connect meaningfully with his son. All developmental milestones were within normal limits.

Colin had several significant sensory sensitivities. For example, he would cry when he heard loud sounds such as the door bell. His sensitivity, however, gave him pleasure as well. He enjoyed music and pretty colors and was very attentive to even small visual changes in his environment. Mrs. S. remembers Colin at age one as a "laughing baby" who was loving and "always happy." Mrs. S. also remembered how emotionally connected and responsive Colin seemed at two years to an interviewer at a nursery school program.

Shortly after Colin's second birthday, his family planned a five day trip abroad, but Colin became ill before their departure. Colin and his mother stayed behind and his father and grandmother both left for Europe. During their absence, as mother reported, "Colin became inconsolable and cried until his father and grandmother returned." Mother, too, became angry and upset.

Both parents agree that Colin's behavior changed at this point in time. He became both more anxious and extremely sensitive to all separations. The change became magnified when he began attending nursery school the following fall. Mrs. S. remembers that Colin seemed very shy and had difficulty adapting. He did not get along with the other children and would hit them if he did not get his way, or else he would scowl, cross his arms, and turn his face to the wall. Simultaneously, he also began to have temper tantrums at home, a new behavior for him and one which exacerbated longstanding parental anxieties about controlling anger and aggression.

His mother, concerned that Colin was too isolated from his peers, decided to have a second child "to provide Colin with companionship." However, when amniocentesis led to the fetal diagnosis of Down syndrome, the couple decided to terminate the pregnancy. Having also discovered that the unborn child was a girl, Mrs. S. named the fetus "Miriam" after a revered teacher. Afterward she felt grateful for a three week delay prior to the abortion as it allowed her, as she put it, "to get to know Miriam." She had fantasies of sewing dresses for her daughter and of giving the child to her mother so that "she would have something to live for." Notably, though her husband experienced a pronounced grief reaction following the abortion, Mrs. S. did not. Moreover, though she felt chronically depressed and anxious thereafter, Mrs. S. did not connect these feelings with the loss of "Miriam," whose ashes continued to reside in an urn in her bedroom closet.

Colin's cross-gender behavior began within weeks after the abortion and it has endured since then. His favorite activities are dressing up as a girl and putting on make-up, playing with Barbie Dolls, and watching video movies of Snow White and Cinderella. Both parents had artistic interests and they viewed his cross-gender behaviors as part of his own artistic and creative nature. Mr. S. did feel somewhat uneasy about his son's preference for female attire and activities, but he did not redirect it because he believed that it was temporary and that Colin would outgrow it. For her part, Mrs. S. did not identify Colin's gender preferences as a matter of concern in any way.

In the months following the abortion, Mrs. S. came to experience Colin's general hypersensitivity and responsiveness as selectively attuned to herself: "He was always tuned into my feelings. He always knew how I felt." She began to call him by a new name, "Lovey," and took a new delight in his "artistic" talents, which now included cross-dressing.

All was not bliss, however. At approximately the same time the cross-gender behavior emerged, Colin's temper tantrums at home began to intensify. Mrs. S. viewed the tantrums in terms of his abandoning her, as a loss of his previously adoring behavior, and as reminiscent of his biting her nipples at eight months. It was only after years of therapy, however, that she was able to remember how strongly she would censure these outbursts by the boy. She would shake Colin and yell at him full-face. In therapy she recalled that while shaking him she would "look into his eyes and realize that he was afraid that I might kill him."

Discussion:

Colin presented with the driven, exclusive interest in cross-gender behaviors typical of boys with GID. Other collateral features, such as separation anxiety, maternal trauma, parental tolerance for the cross-gender symptoms, heightened sensory sensitivities, and avoidance of rough-and-tumble play with peers (but not with his father) were also typical for the disorder.

As a newborn and as a small infant Colin had successfully managed to form a close, mutually satisfying relationship with his mother despite his special sensitivities. However, he was less successful in forming an early tie to his father who, despite looking forward to having a son, felt himself excluded from the mother-infant dyad and withdrew from both his son and his wife. Colin's further separation from his father at age two — at a time when the marriage was under great stress— seems to have made him separation-anxious, in part because of its collateral impact on his mother. When six months later his mother entered into a period of depressed withdrawal following the abortion of "Miriam," Colin was left to his own resources, this at a time when his cognitive development had made the distinction between boy and girl newly salient. Once established, his fantasy of being the opposite gender seems to have helped him cope not only with the withdrawal of his mother, but with other stressful situations as well. During the time when the disorder first became established, Colin's relationship with his mother appears to have shifted from being over-involved to being under-involved (with both occasional hostile exchanges and role reversal noted). Interestingly, though the opportunity was now there, the father did not know how to establish closer contact with either Colin or the mother during the post-abortion period.

The question of a differential diagnosis in this case involved whether Colin's cross-gender behavior was 1) a passing phase (as sometimes occurs in relation to severe familial stress), 2) an indication of gender non-conforming interests, or 3) an indication of a gender identity disorder. At the time of referral the cross-gender behavior had been ongoing with great intensity for over one year (well beyond the three-month period that qualifies as the outer limit for a passing phase brought about by family stress). Moreover, his cross-gender fantasies and behavior revealed a preoccupation of great emotional intensity and persuasiveness. The behavior did not qualify as simple gender non-conformity — first, because it did not show the range, flexibility, and enjoyment that one would expect, and second, because the cross-gender fantasies were connected intrapsychically to the child's management of distress, separation anxiety, and aggression, and appeared etiologically to be linked to the disruption of his primary attachment relationship.

Intervention:

Colin requires intensive individual psychotherapy, at a minimum of three times a week. Joint play sessions would also help the parents learn to use symbolic play to help Colin deal with his preoccupations and find ways to express his feelings in play. In the play setting, Colin could experiment with different roles and the expression of the more assertive and aggressive aspects of life. This intensive treatment approach would be crucial during the next three to four years of Colin's life, during which time his sense of self will still be forming and consolidating.

In addition, collateral sessions with his parents would be needed to discuss his behavior, the meaning of his play, and day-to-day caregiving approaches, as well as other issues of concern to the parents. Individual psychotherapy for the parent(s) would also be indicated to help them deal with their feelings and relationship to their son, as well as each other. It would be especially important to facilitate a great deal of security and respect in Colin's relationship with his mother and a great deal of interaction, closeness, and relaxed play with his father. Colin should be seen by an occupational therapist for evaluation to determine whether he needs treatment and/or whether his parents could benefit from guidance about activities to support sensory-motor development. Colin could attend a therapeutic nursery program where his individual psychotherapy could be integrated into the program, or enroll in a small preschool program where he would have the opportunity to make friends with children in his community.

Diagnostic Impression:

Axis I: Gender Identity Disorder
Axis II: Underinvolved Relationship
Axis III: None
Axis IV: Psychosocial Stressor—Moderate effects
Axis V: Functional Developmental Level — Has achieved age-expected level with marked constrictions and instability.

Case 14: Steve

Case Description:

Thirty-month-old Steve was referred by a program for parents with addiction problems which his mother, Cindy, attended. Steve was very delayed in speech, with concurrent delays in fine motor, cognitive, language and self-help skills, but above average in gross motor skills. He was not yet toilet trained and was viewed as being "orally fixated," in that everything went into his mouth; he sucked his thumb, stuck out his tongue, and drooled. but avoided touching certain textures. He had difficulty calming himself down and was over-reactive to sudden noises, which alarmed him.

His mother's concerns focused on his aggressive behaviors, angry outbursts, and their historic lack of connectedness. When angry he would say, "Mommy, I need to bite". At home he demonstrated extreme tantruming and destructive behavior though he could respond when his mother set appropriate limits. During Steve's first two years of life, both parents abused alcohol and drugs and had a very conflictual partner/parent relationship. Cindy acknowledged her lack of emotional availability to Steve and her neglect and physical abuse towards him, as well as his experience of her physical aggression towards his father.

Steve was the produce of an unexpected and unplanned pregnancy. Until Cindy was eight weeks pregnant, she was actively using cocaine, valium, alcohol, and marijuana. Upon discovering that she was pregnant, she discontinued use of all drugs except marijuana, which she used at a rate of four joints a day.

Cindy described Steve as being a fussy child from birth: he was sensitive to sudden loud or vibrating sounds, cried when he was changed or dressed, was fearful when moved in space, and could not calm himself down. She described feeding difficulties, with several switches of formula before finding one he could tolerate. Steve continued to be a poor eater and was only at the tenth percentile on growth charts. Steve was somewhat slow on gross motor milestones, sitting at nine months and walking at eighteen months. He also exhibited significant delays in speech, with his first words at 18 months of age. Steve has a history of ear infections, and was quite sick with pneumonia. A hearing test was performed but results were not conclusive.

Due to some of the oral behaviors and the lability of his mood and angry outbursts, Steve was also referred for a neurological assessment and was found to be normal. Findings from this assessment indicated that Steve's behavioral or developmental concerns were more aptly explained by early environmental influences.

During a structured assessment of the parent-child interaction, Cindy's affect was generally constricted throughout her interactions with Steve. Her speech had a controlled, lilting quality, sounded artificial, and had hostile-sounding edge. She seemed very attuned to Steve's performance, such as his opening the box of raisins or pouring the juice. Cindy used eye contact infrequently and lacked a strong repertoire of ways to engage or reengage Steve in a task. During the feeding segment Cindy exhibited a great deal of passivity and boundary confusion, often asking Steve if she could eat her snack. There was no shared sense of "joie de vivre" and not much conversation around their activities.

During the structured play time, Cindy became more engaged with her son. It was clear that she was attempting to utilize special play techniques which she had learned at the center. However, she was unable to follow Steve's lead in play. She was overly intrusive, attempting to direct and control his play. In looking at Cindy and Steve's dyadic interaction, the examiner found that the affective quality was generally empty except for periods when Cindy was attempting to exert control; then mother and son would both be irritable. There was often joint attention to a task but no sense of reciprocity. Steve appeared anxiously attached to his mother; he protested upon her departure from the room but turned away from her, without seeking comfort, upon her return.

Both parents' interactional styles with Steve were characterized by tenseness, a striving for control, and a general lack of emotional expression. Cindy appears to have intense emotions lying under the surface. The father exhibited several instances of appropriate redirection with Steve as well as attending to joint activities. Cindy could soften her voice, giving it the qualities of "motherese"; however, she did so infrequently. The tone of her voice was generally harsh and demanding.

Discussion:

Steve presented many of the motor and sensory patterns characteristic of infants born to mothers who have abused drugs during pregnancy. The over-reactivity to sounds and touch, the irritability, the poor eating (oral-motor sensitivity), and the poor self-regulation and self-comforting are also consistent with hypersensitive Regulatory Disorder. He was a challenging infant at best, but coupled with the deprivation and abuse in his environment, he started to develop negativistic and defiant behaviors to engage the world. It is evident that Steve's behavioral difficulties are intensified by the interaction between him and his mother. This was characterized by a striving for control, a general lack of emotional expression, and overly intrusive behavior. These interactive behaviors are severely disturbed. Mother's difficulties are also evident in her inappropriate demands (i.e toilet training, requiring Steve to be her "little man"), and attempts to involve Steve in meeting her own needs. Her perceptions of Steve include diffuse boundaries which reflect a lack of consistency, including periods of romanticized interactions and periods of anger. The regulatory features take precedence for Axis I and the interactive factors are captured in Axis II.

Intervention:

In this case it would be easy to get lost in the challenges of the relationship problem, but the diagnosis points to the importance of taking into account

Steve's regulatory difficulties as a way to help improve the interaction patterns. The psychotherapist would need to address the specific implications of the regulatory difficulties, help the dyad interact more successfully and pleasurably, and work through their earlier disappointments. In addition, occupational therapy is indicated and should include a home program that the parents could implement to help Steve cope more adaptively day to day as he improved. Daily developmentally-based play sessions would provide the ongoing support to facilitate Steve's development and relationships.

Diagnostic Impression:

Axis I: Regulatory Disorder — Type I Hypersensitive
Axis II: Overinvolved Relationship
Axis III: Developmental Expressive Language (DSM IV)315.31
Axis IV: Psychosocial Stress—Moderate effects
Axis V: Functional Emotional Developmental Level - At expected level but with constrictions

Case 15: Suzy

Case Description:

Suzy came for an evaluation at 26 months, several months after her brother's birth, because of an increase in negative "overly sensitive" behavior. She was waking three or four times during the night, did not seem happy, was strong willed, and broke down in tears quickly, as things never seemed quite right or quick enough for her. Mother noted Suzy was very cold to her and would often ignore her when she returned from her part-time work, but Suzy could be happy and outgoing sometimes and had gifted intelligence, was very verbal, loved to be read to, and could be happy playing with friends. She also enjoyed the sandbox and occasionally took nice walks with her mother.

The developmental history included a normal pregnancy and delivery. Suzy was a healthy eight-pound infant. Mother did not work during the first five months, but indicated there had been fighting between herself and her husband, who had a drinking problem, during Suzy's first year. During her first three months Suzy was irritable and colicky, and she still tended to get easily overstimulated by sights and sound, requiring long periods of rocking and holding to settle her down. She evidenced a warm and engaging smile by 3-4 months, but was easily distracted by noises. Between 4-10 months she was assertive and demanding, with lots of fussy times.

It was not until she walked, at 14 months, that she had a two-month period of great joy, controlling her mobility and discovering the house. Mother continued to feel unrewarded as she felt her daughter walk away from her, but they did have happy moments together, when Suzy sat on her lap and read books. However, at 16 months, they entered a negative phase, as Mother grew more tired from a second pregnancy and fighting increased with her husband, who was drinking more.

Father saw himself as a person who controlled himself and tended to be passive and avoid confrontation or conflict, but would drink when he got anxious. He was "happy" to see his daughter but would withdraw or get annoyed if she was demanding and showed strong emotion. Mother said that her daughter's demandingness made her feel "empty inside" and vacillated between frenetically trying to make her happy and becoming controlling and annoyed with her. When she played with Suzy, she was tense and mechanical, expressing very little emotion. Suzy, very bright and verbal, could develop pretend play, but she was very solemn and marching to her own drummer rather than interacting with her mother. As Suzy tuned her out, Mother looked puzzled and somewhat paralyzed by anxiety, unable to jump in and join her daughter's drama. Father was more intrusive, rather than avoidant, but Suzy pushed him away as they interacted around the theme of him intruding and her trying to turn him off. When he attempted to "horse around," she screamed angrily, wanting to get back to her toys.

They did communicate with each other, in the sense that she responded to him clearly and logically, and he responded to her cues by trying to take over.

As part of the evaluation, Suzy accepted the clinician's help and set up a pretend play drama. She explained her ideas, becoming more engaged and related as they played. She could stay with long sequences, able to control and limit her impulses even when frustrated, but continued to look serious and sad as she persisted in trying to get her dolls to simply ride the horses. Her play never broadened into themes of curiosity, or exploration, or even anger. She was an organized, intentional and interactive youngster with complex behavior, but she lacked pleasure, joy and spontaneity. Both parents could be logical and organized, but one seemed to be leaving Suzy empty while the other seemed to be trying to control and overload her.

Suzy appeared age-appropriate in terms of her ability to relate and engage, use gestures intentionally, and use early representational modes to communicate. She was able to control her impulses, concentrate, and maintain a relatively even mood. At the same time, there were indications of a rather marked constriction in the range of affect she had available to her, showing little pleasure or spontaneity or creativity. Her history indicated moodiness and lability of affect, and poor frustration tolerance from early infancy. At present she showed constrictions in the flexibility of age-appropriate personality functions with a narrowing of range, particularly in the areas of, pleasure, joy and spontaneity and a tendency toward greater lability of moods.

Discussion:

Several elements may be considered in this case. Suzy manifested individual differences as an infant in mild sensitivities to sound and touch, which resulted in some irritability and difficulty calming, as well as a tendency toward labile moods. She and her parents had difficulty interacting with each other, resulting in the lack of pleasure and spontaneity, and constriction of overall affect. With maturation, these individual differences resolved, and later Suzy did not appear anxious or fearful, had developed good motor, cognitive and language abilities, had friends, and did not exhibit the moodiness and reactivity described in her earlier history during the current evaluation. Most salient were the constricted range of emotional expression and reduced affective range, conveyed in part through her persistent negativistic and dissatisfied feelings. The parent-child relationship was tense and unhappy. Although she was having sleep difficulties, these did not appear primary. While maturation seemed to have resolved the individual differences and they had not become regulatory difficulties, Regulatory Disorder should be considered in the differential diagnosis.

Intervention:

Maturational factors had already worked in Suzy's favor, but she remained an unhappy child with significant constrictions. Three components would be indicated in the intervention. One, parent guidance would help the parents find ways to give Suzy a "vote" through which she could still exercise some control by making a choice rather than rejecting everything outright. In addition, her parents need to learn how to help her through transitions when many conflicts occur, as well as how to be more objective about things which need to be done (e.g., "Look at the time") and limit setting. Praise and rewards for appropriate behavior, specifying what made what she did so wonderful (e.g., "You looked at all of the pieces before you started," "You waited to see if we were ready before opening the door") would also boost Suzy's self-esteem and sense of competence. Two, brief psychotherapy would help parents work through their feelings of inadequacy, rejection and anger or disappointment. This would allow them to overcome their own constrictions in order to be able to reach out and follow her lead as well as have fun together. Three, joint play sessions would be especially important, given Suzy's constricted affect, to encourage more symbolic expression of her feelings and to experiment with a broader range of feelings safely. Because of her tendencies to tune out and reject her parents' responses, they would need to follow her lead sensitively and respect the control she could have in play, as she tested their acceptance of her wishes, fears, impulses and other feelings. These sessions would support daily interactive play (i.e., "floor time") at home and would lead to more reflective conversations. The intervention would not need to be very long, but it is important to include all three components with follow up consultation at the next developmental challenges.

Diagnostic Impression:

Axis I: Disorder of Affect - Mixed Disorder of Emotional Expressiveness
Axis II: While the relationship is significantly anxious and tense, it is not so disturbed to constitute a disorder.
Axis III: None
Axis IV: Psychosocial Stressors - Mild effects
Axis V: Functional Emotional Developmental Level - At expected representational level with constrictions

Case 16: Tommy

Case Description:

Thirty-six-month-old Tommy walked clumsily into the room, looked around, glanced quickly at the examiner, and began to wander aimlessly around the room, taking no notice of the examiner or toys in the room. While he wandered, there was a sense of emotional connectedness to his parents, but an indirect one. He didn't look at them and make eye contact, and he didn't exchange gestures with them.

After a few minutes of wandering, some islands of purposeful activity began to emerge. He picked up a pop-up toy and began to press it with his father's help. He tried to open the door of the office to leave, but turned away when told, "No, don't touch that!" but did not vocalize or even look at this parents, and just wandered to something else. As he walked around, he made lots of high-pitched squeals and sounds, but there were no distinct syllables or babbles. Mother looked depressed and tired as she offered him a fire truck, which he took from her and looked at before dropping it to the floor and wandering off again.

Mother tended to follow Tommy's lead and be responsive and contingent, even though he ignored her. She also responded to his gestures with animation and availability. When Tommy wanted to open the door latch, they exchanged some gestures and looks but he could not imitate her opening it. His father was more tense, tried to structure things and take over, suggesting one thing after another as he pulled Tommy into ring-around-the-rosie, catching a ball, and reading a book. Tommy was pulled along, but had no way to take the lead while father was so busy introducing new subjects. As soon as he could, he wandered away, tuning his father out. He used no words or intentional-type babble, other than sounds of frustration. He finally pointed to his mother's bag and when she approved, took out a cookie. As he ate, he showed nice organized contact with his father and even gave him a cookie when asked. He relaxed, making a number of focused gestures toward his father, and some warm smiles. In general, Tommy's style was to engage a little and then disengage, aimlessly wander around and then reengage.

The pregnancy and delivery of Tommy had been uneventful. He was very alert the first two months of life, awake ten to twelve hours a day, and was a very easy baby. He loved to look around, enjoyed music, and loved rough, brisk movement. He also liked all kinds of touch. He was always a good sleeper and eater and seemed more curious and related than most babies, following his mother's voice and face, and responding to her gestures. He loved to play peek-a-boo and once he was able to crawl came charging across the room to play a football game with his dad.

At one year, he appeared to be a sensitive, bright, verbal and alert little boy, who was highly cautious of new experiences and new people. Father revealed that Tommy's temperament was very much like his own and that he had a history of anxiety and avoidance, which had required treatment. Mother did not have a psychiatric history, nor did either of the parent's families. Mother returned to work part-time when Tommy was eight months old and stopped again, when he was 14 months, to get pregnant again. Tommy had a steady caregiver and had gotten to know his grandmother very well.

As a toddler, Tommy loved to look at pictures. He was the "shy observer" type in his relations with other children but would warm up slowly and join them. At 21 months he had many words and could play interactive games. At about this time, he had a series of ear infections, leading to many rounds of antibiotics. He gradually became more anxious and frightened, with repetitious nightmares and daytime fears of strangers, new children, and even clowns. When he was 24 months old, his sister was born, and he cried jealously when she was held. He cried bitterly when he saw her and tried to push and hit her. Tommy gradually began losing his speech and became more withdrawn. He lost interest in toys and books and spent more time in a hyperkinetic remote stare. A series of physical, neurologic, and metabolic tests were done, but all findings were negative. Tommy retained his understanding of day-to-day directions and minimal gesturing, but most of the time he spent running back and forth, jumping, flapping, wringing his hands and shouting without any purpose.

Discussion:

The etiology of Tommy's deterioration is elusive, but one can postulate three general factors: a mild to moderate constitutional-maturational vulnerability, the psychological stress around his sister's birth, and some possible intervening physiologic stress associated with the middle ear infections and continuous use of antibiotics. The nature of Tommy's symptoms, given his good early development, raises more questions than it answers (and is not that infrequent).

There are some positive factors in the situation, in that Tommy retained his affection toward his parents and his ability, when highly motivated, to organize things at a 14-16-month-old level. At present, however, he shows involvement in multiple areas of development with significant impairment in the processing of sensations as well as in maintaining communication and relatedness.

Intervention:

Tommy will benefit from a very intensive intervention program which addresses the multiple aspects of his disorder. These include sensory processing difficulties, relating and communicating, and learning (with respect to language and cognition). To provide the support for sensory processing, Tommy will need occupational therapy with a sensory integration focus three times a week. In addition, parents should be instructed in developing a home program which provides ongoing support for engaging Tommy in regulating activities (e.g., swinging, jumping on a trampoline or mattress, frequent brushing, etc.). He should also receive speech therapy three times a week and be evaluated further for his reactivity to sound.

There should also be an intensive program to increase Tommy's relatedness by following his lead, treating what he does purposefully, making it necessary for him to increase his gestural communication by "playing dumb" or getting in his way, and working on opening and closing circles of communication to help Tommy interact more consistently on a "two way street." These efforts need to be very intensive, because Tommy does not organize learning experiences for himself, except for meeting some primary needs such as getting food . It is important that Tommy not have "down time," i.e., time in which he is passively watching videos or not interacting with others or engaged in purposeful activity. As Tommy responds to these initial efforts, there will be opportunities to open the door to more symbolic learning through words and pretend play as he becomes more related. Depending on progress with the above approaches, an additional assessment should be considered. If progress is not dramatic, simultaneously with the above program, a more structured, intensive one-to-one learning program using reinforcement techniques should be considered to help Tommy learn to follow directions, imitate actions, do cognitive tasks, use language, etc. This part of the intervention could be carried out at home or within a special education program. The education program should also include contact with children who are communicative and interactive in order to allow Tommy to learn from others with the mediation of a teacher or assistant.

Diagnostic Impressions

Axis I: Multisystem Developmental Disorder

Axis II: No Relationship Classification

Axis III: None at this time

Axis IV: Psychosocial Stressors — Moderate effects

Axis V: Functional Emotional Developmental Level — Has not achieved current level and has lost prior levels

Case 17: Marvelle

Case Description:

Marvelle is the 38-month-old biracial daughter of Janice (age 22) and Mr. R. (age unknown). Janice is unemployed, receives AFDC, and functions within the borderline intellectual range. She was in special education classes and did not complete high school. Janice also has a history of emotional difficulties, including verbal explosiveness and physical aggression toward others, sexually inappropriate behavior (e.g. masturbating in her foster mother's presence), and suicidality. She was in multiple foster placements as a child and adolescent, and spent two years in residential treatment, followed by a psychiatric hospitalization during which she was diagnosed as having a Borderline Personality Disorder and Dysthymic Disorder.

Janice was referred for a court-ordered evaluation of her parenting capacity and an assessment Marvelle. The referral was made following an incident in which Marvelle sustained second and nearly third-degree burns to her feet while left for approximately two months in the care of the mother of one of Janice's acquaintances, Ms. C., because Janice's apartment building did not allow children.

During the assessment, Janice spoke frequently to Marvelle, but her comments tended to be repetitions of directions. Janice tended to use an angry and hostile tone of voice, and showed little positive affect unless engaged in unstructured play. Her approach during the structured task lacked enthusiasm, and she expressed little enjoyment or pleasure in being with her daughter.

Janice was abrupt in her handling of Marvelle and was at times intrusive, tickling her repeatedly. She and Marvelle did show some warm cuddling at the end of the initial interview, however. Janice's eye contact with Marvelle was essentially limited to times in which she was reprimanding or directing her; no positive visual regard was noted. Moreover, it was particularly difficult for Janice to take the role of adult caretaker in a manner appropriate to Marvelle's developmental needs and the task at hand. She was limited in her ability to teach Marvelle, demonstrate and give clear expectations about what she wanted her to do, and focus her attention. In addition, Janice showed a tendency to respond contingently to Marvelle's negativistic or non-compliant behaviors, but was less consistent in responding to Marvelle when her behavior was more positive and age-appropriate. She also evidenced difficulty responding to and reflecting Marvelle's feeling states.

Marvelle, in contrast, expressed much positive affect during the assessment, was cheerful in the presence of her mother, and took pleasure in her accomplishments. She showed a capacity to focus on an activity and persist in the face of frustration. At the same time, however, Marvelle impulsively threw the task materials after her mother failed to acknowledge her efforts. She was also observed to engage in a number of avoidance behaviors, such as walking away from Janice, ignoring her directives, and making only fleeting eye contact. In addition, Marvelle showed a fair amount of noncompliance, particularly during the structured task. She played with the task materials in her own way, left the table at which she and Janice were seated, and refused at one point to play with her mother. Furthermore, Marvelle tended to test her mother's limits by waiting until her mother moved toward her in a threatening manner before complying.

As a mother-child dyad, Janice and Marvelle showed a lack of joint attention and mutual engagement. They engaged in little dialogue or turn-taking, and lacked the timing and pacing of events needed to be in sync with one another. There was also a significant discrepancy between Janice and Marvelle's arousal and activity levels, as well as their emotional states. They tended to get "locked" into a rigid, nonreciprocal pattern of communication that is less than satisfying to both of them. Nevertheless, Janice stated that she enjoys being with Marvelle when Marvelle listens to her and when they are playing together. She is most frustrated when Marvelle is noncompliant and when she cannot determine what Marvelle is wanting, needing and feeling. Marvelle reminds Janice of herself, both in appearance and temperament. Janice states that Marvelle gets angry and whines just like she does.

At present, few social supports are available to Janice and Marvelle. Janice no longer lives in the same apartment complex as Ms. C. Janice's only other significant support is her current boyfriend. Their relationship, however, has been quite conflictual, which likely increases, rather than decreases, Janice's overall level of stress.

Discussion:

At age three, Marvelle is a child with a number of special needs. It would appear that her speech and language delays continue, and her social and emotional status is of significant concern. She tends to view others as being both nurturing and aggressive, having observed this pattern in her mother. Marvelle is ambivalent in her interactions with Janice, wanting to engage but simultaneously wanting to distance. She attempts to pull Janice out of her own self-absorption and emotional distress, but then has difficulty tolerating the intensity of Janice's needs and her abusive intrusiveness. Their anxious attachment leads Marvelle to indiscriminately seek out others who might respond to her. The relationship includes both verbal and physical abuse and lacks predictability and boundaries.

As to a primary diagnosis, Marvelle does not present the specific symptoms of a child who has just experienced a trauma, perhaps because her entire life has ben "traumatic," in the sense of persistent physical and verbal abuse. While she does not appear to have developed additional symptoms following being burnt, the persistent neglect, abuse and distorted caregiving patterns have resulted in patterns of approach-avoidance, social indiscriminateness, and angry, defiant behaviors. These are most consistent with Reactive Attachment Disorder.

Intervention:

Given the considerable ongoing risk factors present in this situation, the intervention needs to be both comprehensive and flexible, with emphasis on ongoing therapeutic relationships for both parent and child within a team approach to sustain the intervenor efforts. The program would need home and center based components, including outreach, transportation, education and work incentives, therapeutic groups and individual and parent-child psychotherapy. It would first be necessary to help Janice secure stable living arrangements for herself and daughter, possibly in a group or family home, as well as other basic needs such as food, clothing and medical care. A therapeutic nursery program which included mediated interactive play between parents and children would encourage fun and success together. A parenting group would provide peer support, friendships, guidance and problem solving together. Depending on Marvelle's response to the overall therapeutic support and individual psychotherapy, individual speech and language work may be indicated. The effects of Janice's difficult life and successive failures would need to be worked through this relationship which should be viewed as a long term prospect. The degree to which Janice is able to participate and make use of the various aspects of the program and educational and work incentives for herself will related to the degree to which an individual therapeutic relationship develops and encourages these challenges. Meanwhile, given her age and accumulated distress, Marvelle will also need an individual relationship and a consistent day care situation to help her learn to trust attachments and communicate her needs and feelings without fear of abuse. The individual therapists would also work with the dyad together throughout the recovery process.

Diagnostic Impression:

Axis I: Reactive Attachment Deprivation/Maltreatment Disorder
Axis II: Abusive Relationship — Verbal, Physical
Axis III: Developmental Expressive and Receptive Language Disorders
(DSM IV 315.31)
Axis IV: Psychosocial Stress— Severe effects
Axis V: Functional Emotional Developmental Level — At expected levels
with constrictions

Index to Primary Diagnoses of Cases